Heroes
of
ISRAEL

Other Books in this Series

Heroes of Mexico
Heroes of Puerto Rico
Heroes of the American Indian
Heroes of Science
Heroines of America

Forthcoming

Heroes of Conservation
Heroes of 1776
Heroes of Music
Heroes of Medicine
Heroes of Discovery
Heroes of Archaeology
Heroes of the Civil War
  (2 *volumes*)
Heroes of Journalism
Heroes of American Unionism
Heroes of American Art
Heroes de Puerto Rico
  (*Spanish language edition*)

Heroes of ISRAEL

by

Morris Rosenblum

Fleet Press Corporation
New York

Cover design and title page: Seal of Israel

© Copyright, 1972, Fleet Press Corporation
156 Fifth Avenue
New York City 10010

All rights reserved

Library of Congress Catalog Card Number: 77-100087

Manufactured in the United States of America

No portion of this book may be reprinted in any form without the written permission of the publisher, except by a reviewer who wishes to quote brief passages in connection with a review for a newspaper, magazine, or radio-television program.

ACKNOWLEDGMENTS

For their help in obtaining illustrations thanks are due to Mrs. Marilyn Rosenbluth Frankenthaler; Mrs. Miriam Neeman, Manager of the Archives, Hannah Senesh House, Sdot Yam, Israel; Mrs. Amit Silman of the Israel Office of Information, New York; Miss Esther Togman of the Zionist Archives and Library, New York; Stanley P. Tozetski, Chief, Archives of History Section, United States Military Academy, New York.

This book is dedicated to my wife, Dora, whose help and encouragement are deeply appreciated.

Morris Rosenblum

CREDITS FOR ILLUSTRATIONS

Government of Israel Press Office, Tel Aviv; Hannah Senesh House, Sdot Yam; Israel Information Services, New York; Photo Braun; Morris Rosenblum; United States Military Academy Archives, West Point, N.Y.; Zionist Archives and Library, New York.

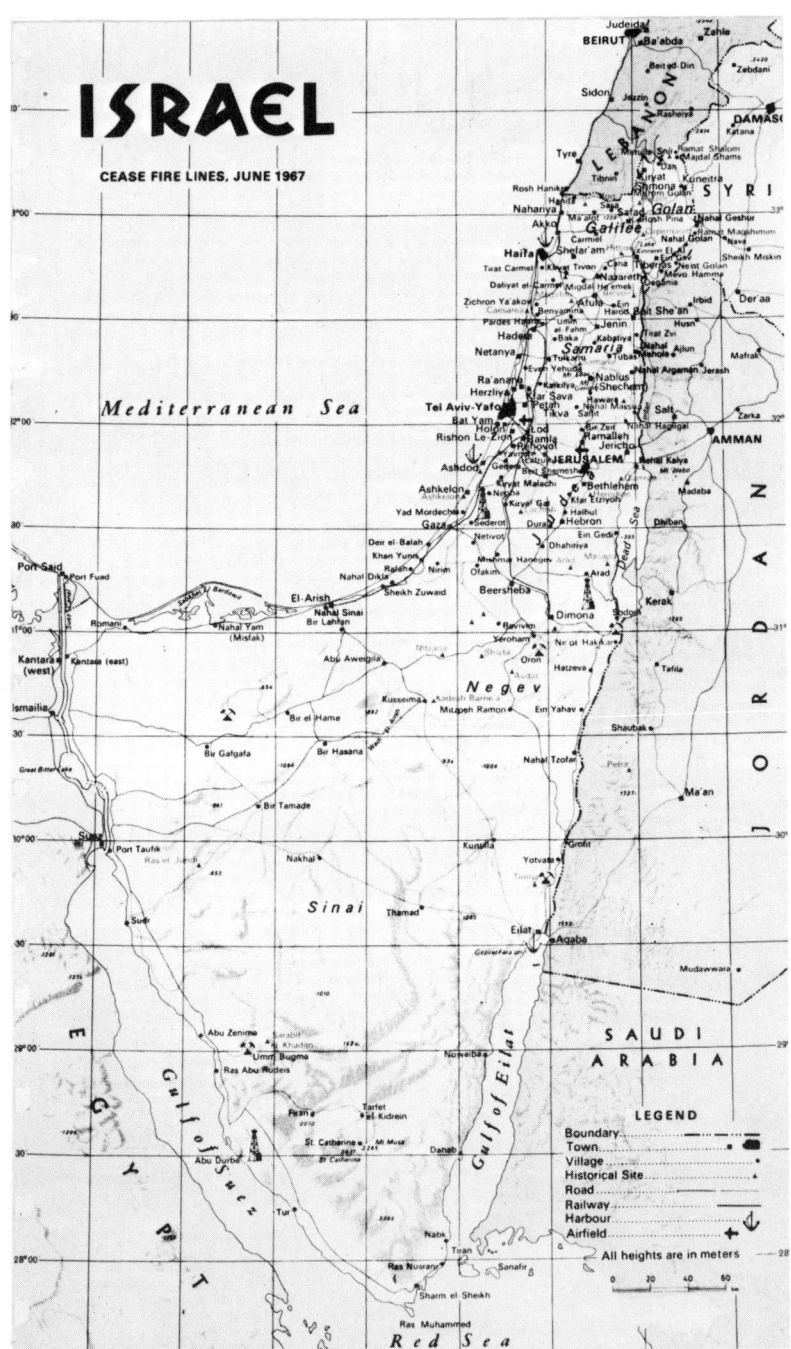

Israel and Occupied Territory

CONTENTS

1. **The Land of Israel**   9
   Heroes, Dispersions, and Return
2. **Theodor Herzl**   19
   A Prophet Whose Dream Came True
3. **Chaim Weizmann**   30
   Israel's First President
4. **David Ben-Gurion**   39
   Pioneer to Prime Minister
5. **Joseph Trumpeldor**   55
   "Never Mind"
6. **Eliezer Ben Yehuda**   62
   "Only Hebrew Spoken Here"
7. **Hannah Senesh**   72
   "Blessed is the Match"
8. **Mickey Marcus**   77
   A Soldier for All Humanity
9. **Yigael Yadin**   86
   Archeologist and Warrior
10. **Yigal Allon**   94
    Redoubtable, Bold and Imaginative
11. **Moshe Dayan**   100
    An Ideal Sabra and Born Leader: "Follow Me!"
12. **Golda Meir**   112
    Israel's First Lady Premier
13. **Shmuel Yosef Agnon**   119
    Israel's Nobel Prize Winner

    Index   125

The Western (Wailing) Wall

The Land of Israel

1 Heroes, Dispersions, and Return

"Israel is a country so tiny that there is no room to write its name on the world map," according to Ephraim Kishon, Israel's leading humorist. In spite of its small size and population, Israel has always been mighty in its accomplishments. In Biblical days and during the period of Greek and Roman occupation, Israel gave to the world a long list of great heroes and heroines. In the short time since the land of Israel once more became the Jewish homeland, it has again presented to the world an impressive list of heroic characters.

The original founder of the nation was Abraham, who led his people westward across the Jordan from Ur in Chaldea (Mesopotamia). The Lord promised Canaan to him and his people in these words:

For all the land which thou seest, to thee will I give it, and to thy seed forever.

The next great hero of the people was Moses, who led them out of slavery in Egypt toward the Promised Land. This deliverance of the Jews, or Hebrews, from Egyptian bondage, is celebrated by the feast of Passover (*Pesach*).

Joshua, who succeeded Moses, led the Jews into the Promised Land and occupied it. Gideon, called the most remarkable and attractive leader of the Old Testament, and Samson, famous for his superhuman strength, were not only warriors but also judges, as the early rulers of the Israelites were called.

After the judges, kings ruled over Israel. Oustanding were David, the killer of the giant Goliath, "the sweet psalmist," the symbol of the ideal ruler, and his son, Solomon, famed for his wisdom and the building of the first Temple.

Prophets inspired the people, taught them a way of life, or even cried out against their faults. Among these wise men were Samuel, Elijah, Isaiah, Ezekiel, Daniel, and Jeremiah.

Israel had her heroines also, like Deborah, a mighty warrior and a wise judge, and Queen Esther, wife of the Persian king Ahasuerus (Xerxes), who delivered her people from destruction. The Feast of Purim celebrates this event.

The deeds or teachings of these and other Biblical heroes and heroines are a living part of the tradition and heritage of the Jewish people. In Israel the Old Testament is studied as history and geography. Military operations are often named after persons and events in the Old Testament; a great Israeli leader may be called "another Gideon" or "a modern Moses."

Another part of the tradition has been the dispersion, also called the Diaspora, from a Greek word meaning a scattering, or sowing, of the Jews from Palestine, and their longing and efforts to return.

The name *Palestine*, from Greek and Latin, is often used for the land in which most of the leading events of the Bible took place; modern Israel is only a small part of it.

Three great dispersions took place in ancient times, the first about 722 B.C., when the Assyrians destroyed the Kingdom of Israel and carried most of its people into exile.

Originally, the Israelites consisted of twelve tribes named after the twelve sons of Jacob, who was also called Israel. These tribes had formed the United Kingdom of Israel, but in 922 B.C., after the death of King Solomon, the kingdom split into two parts. The ten northern tribes formed a new Kingdom of Israel, and the two southern ones, the Kingdom of Judah, later called Judea, a name coming from Greek and Latin.

The Israelites who were taken away by the Assyrians never returned to Israel and lost their identity in a foreign land. They are referred to as the Lost Tribes, and their fate is one of the mysteries of history.

In 598 B.C., the second great dispersion of the Jews began. Nebuchadnezzar, the Chaldean king of Babylon, invaded Judea, and captured and destroyed Jerusalem, including the First Temple. Some of the inhabitants fled to Egypt, but Nebuchadnezzar deported most of the people to the Babylonian empire, allowing only the poorest farmers and workers to remain in Judea.

During this sad period known as the Babylonian Captivity or Exile, the Jews taken to Babylon kept their identity, unlike the Lost Tribes. They strengthened their religious faith; there was a growth of the Torah, or sacred law, and of sacred literature. Most of the exiles longed for a return to Zion, as their homeland was often called after the name of a sacred hill in Jerusalem. The words of the 137th Psalm were forever in their thoughts:

By the rivers of Babylon, there we sat down, yea we wept, when we remembered Zion.

We hanged our harps upon the willows in the midst thereof.

For there they that carried us away captive required of us a song; and they that wasted us required of us mirth, saying, Sing us one of the songs of Zion.

How shall we sing the Lord's song in a strange land?

If I forget thee, O Jerusalem, let my right hand forget her cunning.

If I do not remember thee, let my tongue cleave to the roof of my mouth; if I prefer not Jerusalem above my chief joy.

In 539 B.C., less than 50 years after the beginning of the Babylonian Exile, Cyrus the Great, ruler of Persia, overthrew the Babylonian Empire and allowed the Jews to return to Judea and rebuild Jerusalem. However, some Jews preferred to remain in Babylon, which later became a center of Hebrew culture. Others had migrated to Egypt and to more distant parts of Asia, even as far as India and China.

The Second Temple was built in 516 B.C. Judea developed as a religious state with a High Priest as the ruler. It remained free until Alexander the Great appeared in Asia Minor in 332 B.C. The Jews were given special privileges in Alexandria, a city built by the conqueror; many emigrated to North Africa, and at one time there were about 1,000,000 Jews there.

After the death of Alexander in 323 B.C., his empire was divided among five of his generals. About 160 years later, Antiochus IV Epiphanes, called *Epimanes*, "The Madman," ruled over Syria and Palestine. He tried to root out the Jewish religion and plundered the Temple of Solomon.

The Jews found the will and courage to resist, although they were not equipped to fight against a regular army. Under the leadership of Mattathias, an old priest, and his five sons, called the Maccabees, they revolted in 167 B.C.

After the death of Mattathias, Judas Maccabeus (Judah Maccabee) became the leader and carried on guerrilla warfare successfully. He entered the Temple and rededicated it, an event commemorated by the Feast of Hanukah, "Dedication." After Judah fell in battle in 160 B.C., his brothers carried on the fight until Simon, the last surviving one, gained political independence for Judea in 142 B.C.

In 63 B.C., the Romans under Pompey entered Judea, which lost its independence. The Jews did not have their own state again until 1948. The Romans chose the rulers of Judea, first from among the Maccabees, and then from non-Jews, like Herod the Great. When they did not put a king in charge, they appointed a governor called a procurator.

Florus, one of these procurators, was so cruel and oppressive that the people revolted although they had to contend with the mightiest military power of the ancient world. Fighting with desperate courage, the Jews inflicted a crushing defeat upon the Roman prefect of Syria, who had marched into Palestine to take Jerusalem. Nero, then emperor, sent Vespasian, his ablest general, to fight against the Jews.

It took him two years to occupy the whole countryside and cities, except the mountain fortresses and Jerusalem. When civil war broke out elsewhere in the Roman world, Vespasian hurried to Italy, leaving his son, Titus, in charge.

Vespasian became emperor, and there was peace in the Roman Empire, except in Palestine, where the Jews stubbornly resisted. In the words of Tacitus, the Roman historian, the anger of the Romans was increased because only the Jews had not surrendered!

Titus gathered a tremendous army before the walls of Jerusalem. Led by John of Gischala and Simon Bar Giora, a noted guerrilla fighter, the people inside fought back fiercely. However, the Romans made their way into the city, slaughtered a great number of the inhabitants, set fire to the Temple, and turned Jerusalem into a heap of ruins. In this war, about 500,000 Jews were killed, and many thousands more were sold as slaves.

The Temple destroyed by Titus in 70 A.D. was not actually the same one that had been built after the return of the Jews from the Babylonian Exile. That one had been desecrated by Antiochus IV and had fallen into decay. Herod the Great replaced it in 19 B.C. with what he considered to be a more magnificent building. This Temple has never been restored; a few stones from it and Solomon's Temple are left as part of the Western Wall, once popularly known as the Wailing Wall, a place sacred to the Jews.

The Romans now adopted a very harsh policy toward the Jews in Palestine and other parts of the Roman Empire. Once more the Jews in Judea became so desperate that they revolted. The final spark that ignited the flame of revolt was the fact that Hadrian, who became emperor in 117 A.D., planned to rebuild Jerusalem as a pagan city. Rabbi Akiba Ben Joseph, head of the Jewish community in Palestine, went about secretly stirring up a rebellion. Jewish workers made weapons which were stored in caves. A great military leader, Simon Bar Kochba, "Son of a Star," arose to lead the people in war.

About 200,000 took up arms and were so successful at first that once more the Romans had to send their best general. This time he was Julius Severus, who came all the way from Britain. After many battles, the Jewish army was pinned down in the town of Bethar, which fell in 135 A.D., after a year's siege. Bar Kochba was killed, most of the inhabitants were massacred, and Akiba and other leaders were taken prisoner and cruelly put to death.

The fierce resistance of the Jews in two wars made Roman policy toward them most unbearable. Almost all the Jews left Palestine for communities outside the Roman Empire. The third and last dispersion, the Great Diaspora, began. Earlier, the Jews had settled in the Near and

Far East and in parts of the Roman Empire in Europe and North Africa. In later centuries, they migrated to all parts of the world: North and South America, the Caribbean and Pacific islands, South Africa, Australia, and, of course, every country in Europe.

Wherever they came, with few exceptions, they kept their identity as Jews. They became the People of the Book, the Old Testament. They had a common tradition and heritage of learning and prayers and the knowledge that their ancestors had once lived in their own land.

Throughout the centuries, the closing words of the Passover *seder* service were repeated like a cry of hope, "Next year in Jerusalem." In one form or another, these words were part of some prayers at other times of the year. The hope of a return was ever present, but many thought that it would be realized only when the Messiah came.

After the Romans, Palestine was ruled by a long line of conquerors, the Turks ruling it the longest, from 1515 to 1917. Early in the period of Turkish occupation, Joseph Nassi, who came from Portugal, made an attempt to establish a homeland for the Jews in Palestine. He has been called a true forerunner of Zionism.

Nassi's ancestors had been forced to become converts to Christianity during the early period of the Inquisition, but they and their descendants secretly kept up their Jewish faith. Such Spanish and Portuguese Jews were called Marranos.

Nassi and his family emigrated to Turkey. He became a great favorite of Sultan Selim, who gave him the Aegean Islands as a gift and the title of Duke of Naxos.

Nassi had long wanted to build a Jewish state in Palestine. The Sultan gave him the ruined city of Tiberias as a start. Nassi planted mulberry trees to provide food for silk worms; he also imported wool for the manufacture of clothing. He rebuilt the city in 1565 and provided money and ships for Jews to come there. His death in 1579 put an end to the project.

The movement toward Zionism, the establishment of a Jewish national home in Palestine, began in the second half of the 19th century. Many authors wrote appeals urging the Jews to hold on to their national solidarity and to think of settling in Palestine.

One of these writers, Leo Pinsker, an eminent doctor of Odessa, declared in a celebrated book, *Auto-Emancipation* (1882), that a Jewish nationality must be created. In Vienna, the Russian-born Peretz Smolenskin had been writing for years in *Hashahar*, "The Dawn," a Hebrew newspaper founded in 1868, that the Jews were everlastingly linked to Zion and that all their efforts should be directed to colonizing Palestine.

Title page of *Auto-Emancipation*

Some non-Jewish writers had similar ideas. Laurence Oliphant, a British author, wrote in his book *Land of Gilead* (1880), about the formation of a Jewish colony and actually tried to get land for it in Transjordan.

Even more widely read was the novel *Daniel Deronda* (1874-1876) by George Eliot, who set forth the idea of the creation of a Jewish state in Palestine. Daniel, the hero of the novel, had been born a Jew but was brought up as a Christian. After learning the truth about his birth, he married a Jewish girl, Mirah Cohen, became inspired with Jewish nationalism under her brother's influence, and went with Mirah to live in Palestine.

In France, Alexandre Dumas the Younger, wrote a play, *La Femme de Claude*, "Claude's Wife" (1873), in which a character named Daniel praises the idea of a return to Palestine to set up a Jewish national home. Dumas himself wrote to Baron Edmond de Rothschild that if he were a Jew, he would dedicate himself "to retake possession of the land of my origins and traditions, to rebuild the Temple... ."

In the United States, Emma Lazarus, author of the poem, "The New Colossus." whose words are on the Statue of Liberty, was influenced by the works of Oliphant and Eliot. She had written about her people before, about their great heroes, the Maccabees and Bar Kochba. Now she was deeply moved by the sufferings of the Jews in eastern Europe. In 1883, stirred by an anti-Semitic defense of a Russian pogrom, or massacre of the Jews, she wrote in their defense:

"Blind intolerance and ignorance are now forcibly driving them into that position which they have so long hesitated to assume. *They must establish an independent nationality.*"

Groups were formed to aid in the resettlement of Palestine. The most notable of these organizations was the *Hov'vei Zion*, "Lovers of Zion." The movement spread to many countries, with branches in England and the United States. The Lovers of Zion believed that the Jews must return to the soil and that they must become farmers, not tradesmen.

Some of the Lovers of Zion founded Rishon Le Zion, "The First in Zion." A different group that came to Palestine in 1882 was called the Bilu (Biluim). They were an organization of Russian students who made their way to Palestine with little money but great enthusiasm.

There they faced great hardships. A few found work at low wages in the agricultural school established at Mikveh Israel in 1870 by Dr. Charles Netter of Paris for the Jewish children of Jaffa and Jerusalem. Later, some Biluim found work at Rishon Le Zion, others went to Jerusalem to learn a trade. The Biluim were heroic pioneers, but the movement died out, especially since the authorities in Russia discouraged it as revolutionary.

However, other immigrants arrived, especially from Poland, Rumania, and Russia. Many more colonies were built. Israel has been called a "Miracle in the Desert": the work of this first wave of immigration marked the beginning of the miracle. The pioneers, called *chalutzim,* had to work extremely hard to bring about miracles.

The Turks had not developed the land, which was ravaged in wars and had fallen into decay. The forests had been stripped, and most of the soil was dry and unproductive. Malaria was common because large areas of swampland were infested by disease-bearing insects. Roaming Arabs called Bedouins and other hostile Arabs attacked the settlements. Those Arabs who tilled the soil might own small pieces of land on which they kept a few animals and raised scanty crops. Both they and wealthy Arab landowners were willing to sell land, most of which they thought worthless, to the newcomers, often at fantastically high prices.

Three Jewish philanthropists (givers of donations to needy persons or socially useful organizations) helped the early settlers of Palestine. First was Sir Moses Haim Montefiore (1784-1885), who worked for the improvement of the Jews then living there, founded a school for girls and a hospital in Jerusalem. He also tried to establish an agricultural colony near Tiberias, like Joseph Nassi long before his time.

Baron Moritz Hirsch, also known as Baron Maurice de Hirsch (1831-1896), contributed large sums of money for bettering the conditions of Jews throughout the world. He formed the Jewish Colonization Association (later financed by Baron Rothschild) to assist Jews in emigrating from Europe and Asia to any other part of the world. Baron de Hirsch schools were set up in many countries.

Most help was given by Baron Edmond de Rothschild (1845-1934), head of a banking family in Paris. So great were his contributions that in 1914 he said to Chaim Weizmann, "Without me, the Zionists could have done nothing, but without the Zionists, my work would have been dead."

When he heard about the difficulties that the settlers in Palestine were having, he wanted to help for humanitarian reasons. At that time, he did not favor agitation for a return to Palestine, but he was deeply moved by suffering. He gave money to help the early settlements, such as Rishon Le Zion and Samarine (renamed Zichron Ya'akov). Rothschild sent agents to Palestine to buy land, which he rented to the settlers, but the agents managed the property.

For a long time the Baron did not reveal his name but preferred to be known as the Giver, or Benefactor. He made several trips to

Palestine and fell in love with the country. Since he came from France and his agents were French, he encouraged the growing of grapes for wine. Some of the vineyards are still in operation today.

Baron Edmond de Rothschild is sometimes called "Father of the Yishuv." (*Yishuv* means the Jewish community in Palestine.) Peretz Smolenskin called him the Savior of the House of Israel who laid the cornerstone of its rebirth.

When the first large wave of immigrants arrived in Palestine, there were already about 25,000 Jews there. Most of them were descendants of Jews who had never left the country or who had come hundreds of years before. The newcomers differed from these inhabitants in one important way. They came with the idea of working on the land. The older inhabitants lived for the most part in the cities of Haifa, Hebron, Jerusalem, Safed, and Tiberias. Some earned a living by shopkeeping, as tradesmen, or in the professions, but most of them were deeply religious, devoted to study and prayer, and were supported by contributions from abroad.

Ahad Ha'am

The first great wave of immigration, which brought about 10,000 Jews to Palestine, is known as the First Aliyah. The word *aliyah* means an ascent, a going up, as to the Torah during religious services. To the pioneers it meant a rise from exile to the heights of liberty in their own land, a return home. Each successive wave of immigration has been called an Aliyah.

In spite of the examples of the Lovers of Zion, the Bilu, and other early settlers, further attempts at large-scale immigration fell off as the 19th century ended. Some writers thought that there was too much reliance on the generosity of men like Baron Rothschild. Others thought that a new spirit was needed, one that went beyond the mere settlement of Jews to work on the land.

Among these writers was Asher Ginsberg (1856-1927), who wrote for a Hebrew newspaper in Odessa under the pen name Ahad Ha'am, "One of the People." In an article, "This Is Not the Way," he wrote that the Palestinian movement had marched ahead too rapidly. The settlers were going to Palestine merely to find a better way of life there, but Palestine must become a spiritual and cultural Jewish center, with Hebrew as the language of the people. That was the right way, according to Ahad Ha'am.

However, the man who provided the spark and the spirit was one who had not yet read anything by Ahad Ha'am, Peretz Smolenskin, Leo Pinsker, or any of the others who wrote about Palestine as a national home for the Jews.

That man is Theodor Herzl. The story of his life is taken up in the first of the next twelve chapters, which are about twelve modern heroes and heroines of Israel, the same number as that of the Twelve Tribes of Israel.

Baron Edmond de Rothschild

2

Theodor Herzl
A Prophet Whose Dream Came True

On December 19, 1894, a court-martial of a French army officer, Captain Alfred Dreyfus, began in Paris. He was accused of selling military plans to a foreign power. Captain Dreyfus was found guilty, publicly disgraced, and sentenced to life imprisonment on Devil's Island off the coast of French Guiana in South America.

His case attracted world-wide attention because Dreyfus was a Jew, and many persons looked upon his trial and conviction as acts of anti-Semitism. Some prominent Frenchmen worked to get a new trial for him. One of these was the novelist Emile Zola, who wrote the stirring *J'accuse,* "I Accuse," an attack upon the military authorities who had brought Dreyfus to trial. The documents used against Dreyfus were found to be forgeries.

He was brought back to France and given another trial, but the military establishment sentenced him again. However, he was soon pardoned, but was not restored to the army until 1906; in 1914, he received the decoration of the Legion of Honor.

A brilliant journalist, Theodor Herzl, the Paris correspondent of a Viennese paper, *Neue Freie Presse,* "New Free Press," reported the trial, the treatment of Dreyfus, and the effect on the French people. This episode in French history is called the Dreyfus Affair. In 1899, Herzl wrote about its effect on him, "The Dreyfus trial made me a Zionist."

Theodor Herzl was born on May 2, 1860, in Budapest, Hungary, then part of the Austro-Hungarian Empire. His father was a well-to-do businessman; his mother came from a rich and cultured family. Theodor had a sister, Pauline, to whom he was very devoted.

He received a Hebrew education. When he reached his 13th birthday, his parents celebrated his *bar mitzvah,* as is customary in Jewish families. However, the Herzl family was not very religious or devoted to Judaism.

While at school, Theodor discovered he could write well. At 14, he organized a literary and writing society. The members wrote mostly in German. Theodor contributed columns to a newspaper, wrote poems, and planned future works.

In 1878, he passed the final examinations of the high school, actually a college preparatory school. That same year his sister died of pneumonia, and because of grief, his parents moved to Vienna. Theodor entered the law school of the University of Vienna. Law seemed to be the most practical profession for him, as Jews could rarely reach a high public office in Austria-Hungary, but they could earn a living as lawyers.

Theodor Herzl

The Dreyfus Trial

Theodor continued to write while studying law. In 1880, he began to submit light sketches and personal essays to newspapers. In 1882, one was finally accepted. At the university he was very popular and was invited to join a fraternity which had only two other Jewish members. He lived an elegant social life, went to the theater and opera, and became a master of shooting and fencing.

In March, 1883, his fraternity took part in a festival honoring the composer Richard Wagner, at which Wagner's anti-Semitic ideas were expressed. Herzl resigned in protest, but to humiliate him, the fraternity sent him a notice that he had been expelled.

Herzl had come in contact with anti-Semitism even as a boy in high school; later, he heard crowds shouting anti-Semitic slogans. In 1882, he came across a book on the Jewish question by the philosopher Karl Eugen Dühring in which he expressed what is called racism today and openly called for war against the Jews. This book made a deep impression on Herzl, but he was not yet ready to become involved with the Jewish problem. He thought then that anti-Semitism would not last.

In July, 1883, Herzl passed his final law examinations and was admitted to the bar a year later. Since he was extremely fond of travel, and his devoted parents were able to help him, he first went to Switzerland. In May, 1884, he received his doctorate in law at the University of Vienna, made a trip to Paris, and then came back to serve in the law courts of Vienna and Salzburg.

Although he would gladly have remained in the beautiful city of Salzburg if he could become a judge there, he knew that as a Jew he could not rise to that position. Therefore, he left Salzburg and the legal profession.

He returned to his first love, writing. An article by him won a prize in a competition. He wrote short plays, one of which, *Tabarin,* was produced in New York. Reports of its success made his name known in Europe and brought offers to have his other plays produced and to write for newspapers.

In 1889, he married Julie Naschauer, whom he had met while he was a student in Vienna. They made their home in Vienna, where their first child, a daughter, was born in 1890. She was named Pauline after his beloved sister. They had two other children, a boy and a girl.

In October, 1891, after trips to Paris, the Rhine country, and Spain, Herzl was asked by the *New Free Press* to be its Paris correspondent. He felt that in France he could pass "unrecognized" in the crowd but that in Germany and Austria he always had to tremble because somebody might shout anti-Semitic remarks at him.

Ever since he read Dühring's book, he had been thinking about the Jewish question. The idea of a novel about it filled his mind, but first he wrote a play called *The New Ghetto*. In this play, a Jew named Jacob Samuel utters these last words as he is dying from a wound received in a duel, "I want to get out!.... Out of the ghetto."

Herzl suggested no solution; neither in this play nor in his other writings did he yet see a national home for Jews as a way out of the ghetto. He merely wanted to call attention to the problem but for a long time was unable to find anybody who dared to put the play on the stage. The topic was too disturbing.

Then came the Dreyfus trial. Even two years after it, while Dreyfus was still on Devil's Island, Herzl wrote about the fury of the French mobs, about the anti-Semitism of many Frenchmen that he had not noticed before. He wrote that the crowds shouted, "Down with the Jews!" and not, "Down with Dreyfus!" as if they were condemning all Jews. They were not crying out against what might have been a military betrayal but against Dreyfus because he was a Jew, and through him against all Jews.

If such anti-Semitism could take place in France, with its tradition of "Liberty, Equality, and Fraternity," what hope could there be for the Jews in any country?

Added to all the other incidents of anti-Semitism earlier in his life, the Dreyfus Affair certainly made Herzl move strongly in the direction of Zionism. He came to believe that he had no greater aim in life than to devote himself to the Jewish problem, and that its solution depended on getting a national home for the Jews through a greater plan of action than had ever been tried before.

His thoughts, inner struggles, and activities are set down in a diary that he kept from May, 1895, to the end of his life as a record of everything having to do with his fight for a Jewish homeland.

Theodor Herzl might have spent the rest of his life as a prominent journalist or author. Instead, he devoted himself to a dream which he worked night and day to achieve, facing opposition, refusals, and disappointments. At the same time, he made speeches and wrote articles, essays, stories, letters, and two books on a national home for the Jews.

As a first step, Herzl wrote to Baron de Hirsch, requesting a meeting. They met in the Baron's home in Paris on June 2, 1895. Herzl began to present his plans. He had taken with him 22 pages of notes.

He pointed out that the chief misfortune of the Jews had been that they had no united political leadership and suggested that the Baron could provide it. Herzl found fault with the Baron's system of handing out charity and helping build small colonies. He wanted action

Dr. Max Nordau

Theodor Herzl Stamps

on a much larger scale, calling for a mass emigration of Jews to Palestine, for which men like the Baron would provide the money.

Herzl's manner was confident, bold, and almost aggressive. Baron de Hirsch thought that his ideas were fantastic, and that other rich men would give little money. The interview was cut short after Herzl had read from only six pages of his notes. However, the Baron promised to see him again, but this was their last meeting, for the Baron died the following year.

Meanwhile, Herzl began to put his ideas into a pamphlet, or small book. When he completed it, he showed it to a dear friend, who thought that Herzl had become insane. He advised him to see Dr. Max Nordau, a physician and world-famous writer. When Herzl explained his ideas, Nordau said, "If you are mad, then I am mad. I am on your side." Dr. Nordau (1849-1923) became one of Herzl's strongest supporters.

Feeling that he had been in Paris long enough, Herzl applied to the owners of the *New Free Press* for a change of position. His request was granted. Leaving Paris, he traveled and vacationed on his way back to Vienna where he became literary editor of the *New Free Press.* He went back to Paris where he met influential members of the Jewish community. They would not accept his idea of a Jewish national home.

Then he crossed over to England. With Nordau's help, he met Israel Zangwill (1864-1926), who had already gained fame with the novel, *Children of the Ghetto,* and later wrote *Dreamers of the Ghetto* and the famous play, *The Melting Pot.* Zangwill favored the idea of a Jewish state but did not limit the place to Palestine.

In Feburary, 1896, Herzl's small book was published in Vienna under the title *Der Judenstaat*, "The Jewish State." Its appearance created a sensation. Some readers thought that Herzl was a madman or that his idea of a Jewish state was a bad joke. On the other hand, he found many supporters. Dr. Nordau called the book a "masterly deed." The Reverend William Hechler, chaplain to the British Embassy in Vienna, became very enthusiastic and did all he could to help Herzl.

The Jewish State is a beautifully written book, which in about 80 pages sets forth the Jewish problem, proposes a national home as a solution, and then gives Herzl's detailed plan for the structure of the new state. The book was not intended to be just a dream but was a serious attempt to place before the world the idea that the Jews were one people and had a national identity.

As if he were prophesying some future actions of the League of Nations and the United Nations, not yet existing at that time, he wrote that the "Jewish question" had to be established as an international political problem "to be discussed and settled by the civilized nations of the world in council."

At the close of the book, Herzl speaks with the eloquence of the prophets of old:

Therefore I believe that a wondrous breed of Jews will spring up from the earth. The Maccabees will rise again.

Let me repeat once more my opening words: The Jews who will it will achieve their state.

The world will be liberated by our freedom, enriched by our wealth, magnified by our greatness.

And whatever we attempt for our own benefit, will redound mightily and beneficially to the good of all mankind.

After *The Jewish State* was printed, Herzl read for the first time *Rome and Jerusalem (1862)* by Moses Hess and Leo Pinsker's *Auto-Emancipation,* both of which had urged the creation of a Jewish state. Herzl remarked that if he had read Pinsker's book earlier, he might never have written his own book. It is just as well that he had not read any of the books on the idea of a Jewish state. He came to his own writing with a fresh point of view, unsurpassed enthusiasm, and a gripping plan of action. *The Jewish State* aroused greater interest and enthusiasm than all the other books on the same topic.

Herzl now undertook practical measures to gain Palestine. Since it was part of the Turkish Empire, which was heavily in debt, he thought that the Sultan, Abdul Hamid, could be persuaded to sell it. The Reverend William Hechler had interested Grand Duke Friedrich of Baden, a friend of Kaiser Wilhelm II of Germany, in Herzl's project. Herzl asked the Duke to support the idea publicly and to get the Kaiser to see him and also to speak to the Czar of Russia. Herzl wanted these rulers to persuade the Sultan to sell Palestine, but he was unable to get the Duke to act at that time.

However, Herzl persisted because the Sultan's financial condition was getting worse. First, Herzl approached Sir Samuel Montagu, a British banker, who was also a Zionist, but in vain. Then he met Baron Edmond de Rothschild in Paris, but after two hours of discussion, Herzl could not convince him. Rothschild had no faith in Turkish promises and did not think that mass emigration could be controlled in an orderly way.

Unable to make any progress, Herzl wrote in his diary in October, 1896, that he had frankly lost hope. Max Nordau suggested that he organize the masses and recruit those Jews who were the real sufferers. At first, Herzl was against setting "the masses in motion by unorganized unrest." However, he saw no other way of accomplishing his purpose than by organized and unified action.

He therefore issued a call for a meeting of Jewish representatives from all countries. On August 29, 1897, the historic First Zionist Congress met in Basle, Switzerland, with Theodor Herzl as President and Max Nordau as Vice-President; there were about 200 delegates.

Herzl was a striking figure as he addressed the Congress. Tall and broad-shouldered, with a long black square-cut beard, black hair, and dark eyes, he was a dignified and towering leader who looked to some like an Assyrian king, and to others, like a descendant of the House of David. Some delegates felt that they were in the presence of a miracle, of the Messiah himself! They applauded for 15 minutes. Nordau, who followed him, made a brilliant speech, and he, too, was greeted by an ovation.

A plan of action called the Basle Program was adopted: the Zionist Organization was formed; plans were drawn up for the collection of a National Fund and for setting up a Jewish Colonial Bank. The aim of Zionism was defined: "to create for the Jewish people a home in Palestine secured by public law."

Among his impressions of the Basle Congress, Herzl wrote: "If I were to sum up the Basle Congress in one sentence — which I shall not do publicly — it would be this: at Basle I founded the Jewish state. If I were to say this in public today, I would be greeted by the laughter of all. In five years, perhaps, and certainly in fifty, everyone will see it. The State is already founded, in essence, in the will of the people."

The State of Israel was founded only some months after the 50 years that Herzl had set. So highly was his contribution regarded that when the provisional government met on May 14, 1948, to declare that the State of Israel existed, David Ben-Gurion ordered that a picture of Theodor Herzl should be put up in the room where the declaration was being made.

In 1896, Herzl had been told by his family doctor that he was suffering from heart disease brought on by overwork and emotional strain. After the First Congress he thought that he could turn over the leadership to Dr. Nordau and he himself would carry on his literary work, encouraged by the first production of *The New Ghetto*. Dr. Nordau urged him to stay on because he and other Zionists thought that only Herzl could lead the movement.

Herzl finally obtained an audience with Kaiser Wilhelm II with the help of the Grand Duke of Baden, who had become interested in Zionism. In 1898, accompanied by four friends, Herzl met the Kaiser in Constantinople, and in October of the same year, he traveled to

Palestine where he again met the Kaiser. Nothing came of these meetings, although the Kaiser was cordial. In 1901, Herzl met the Sultan himself, who was weak and so under the control of his officials that he could do nothing.

In 1902, while Herzl was in England, his father died, and Herzl rushed back to Vienna to attend the funeral. Herzl keenly felt the disappointment of not having been with his devoted and beloved father in his last moments. Because of his Zionist activities he saw little of his own family, and was hardly ever at home for long periods. He had written in his diary on May 2, 1901:

"It will soon be six years since I began this movement, which has made me old, tired, and poor."

During Herzl's lifetime there were six Zionist Congresses, and in between each Congress, there were meetings of the Action Committee, all of which he attended. During all this time, he still worked for the *New Free Press*, sending articles from the different places he visited. He also carried on a large correspondence, received letters from many countries, and went to see important persons — Jewish leaders, heads of states, and their officials. In addition to those already mentioned, he met ministers of Czar Nicholas II, King Ferdinand I of Bulgaria, King Victor Emmanuel III of Italy, the Papal Nuncio, and Pope Pius X himself.

King Ferdinand and King Victor Emmanuel had nothing but praise for Herzl but were unable to help him. Personal attacks continued, but Herzl also gained the love and admiration of millions all over the world. Only death could stop him from working to reach his goal.

Once more he put this goal down in a book, a novel called *Altneuland*, "Old New Land," published on October 1, 1902. Under its title he wrote words similar to those he had used in *The Jewish State*:

"If you really want it, it is no dream."

Old New Land is like a piece of science fiction, but Herzl did not mean it to be a fantasy. It is the story of two men who visit Palestine on their way to the South Sea Islands to escape from modern civilization. They see a desolate land, but settlements like Rishon Le Zion and Rehovoth offer a ray of hope. Twenty years later, they return, see Palestine again, and are amazed at the changes. With the vision of a prophet, Herzl foresaw the Israel of the future, a land of progress, rebuilt with the aid of science and technology.

In the novel, Herzl put the accomplishment of the dream in 1923, some years ahead of the actual realization. In many details, however, he was a prophet whose dream came true. The title *Tel Aviv*, "Hill of Spring," was used for the Hebrew translation of *Old New Land*. The city of Tel Aviv, built after his death, was like a city he had described in his dream of the future.

The British Government offered some possible sites. Herzl was interested in Cyprus, if Palestine could not be obtained. Sinai was inspected, but the land was found unsuitable, especially because of a shortage of water. Finally, the British made an offer of a place in eastern Africa. This offer is always referred to as the Uganda offer. Herzl was not receptive to it at first.

In April, 1903, the pogrom, or massacre, of Jews in Kishinev, Russia, took place. The need of a Jewish home became more urgent. In August of the same year, the Sixth Zionist Congress met in Basle, with about 600 delegates present, the largest number yet to attend. More than half of them came from Russia.

The most important matter before the Congress was the British offer of Uganda. Herzl explained it and admitted, "Uganda is not Palestine and never could be. It is only a substitute." He realized that Palestine was unobtainable at the moment and thought that Uganda would be a temporary refuge for those Jews who could get out of countries where their lives were in danger. There was bitter opposition, but Dr. Nordau supported his stand, and a majority of the delegates were willing to send a committee to examine the possibility.

The Russian delegates, whose people stood to lose the most in their own country, walked out of the meeting. Herzl got them to return by assuring them that Uganda would be forgotten, and in his closing speech, he uttered the words that had become like a vow:

"If I should forget thee, O Jerusalem, let my right hand forget her cunning."

The stormy meeting was a bitter blow to Herzl. His heart ailment grew worse. He received another blow when his dear friend and loyal follower, Dr. Max Nordau, was shot at by a fanatic, who exclaimed, "Death to Nordau, the East African!" Herzl wrote, "The road is split and the split leads through the leader's heart."

Nevertheless, he carried on to the end. His doctors ordered him to take a complete rest, but he refused in these words, "There is too much to do. Being a Zionist means making sacrifices." Finally, he had to go to a resort for a rest cure, but he did not rest completely. He wrote letters and received visitors to discuss Zionist affairs. Still weak, he returned to Vienna, and then went to the mountain resort of Edlach, where he died on July 3, 1904, only 44 years old.

He was buried in Vienna on July 7, 1904. Millions mourned him all over the world. Tributes to his greatness and magnetism as a leader poured in from Zionists, state officials, princes, kings, and statesmen.

The streets of Vienna were thronged with people of all ages weeping at the passing of a great and beloved man. There was no funeral speech, but spontaneously, the crowd cried out these words as a memorial to him:

"If I forget thee, O Jerusalem, let my right hand forget her cunning."

Nor did Jerusalem forget Theodor Herzl, who has been called "The Father of the Jewish State." He had expressed the wish that if he were not alive when Israel came into being, he should be buried there. In 1949, one year after the creation of Israel, David Ben-Gurion, Prime Minister of Israel, and Dr. Chaim Weizmann, its first President, remembered Herzl's wish.

His body was flown to Tel Aviv and then taken to Jerusalem, where it now rests on Mt. Herzl, a height named after him. Nearby is a military cemetery in which heroes who gave their lives in combat for the freedom of Israel are buried. Like them, Theodor Herzl had given up his life in the same struggle, although he had never fired a shot in war.

Herzl's Tomb

3

Chaim Weizmann
Israel's First President

The distant sound of guns could be heard by a group of men gathered on Mt. Scopus in Jerusalem for a special ceremony on July 24, 1918. Chaim Weizmann, head of a Zionist Commission sent to Palestine, was about to see the first part of a dream he had had since his college days come true: the founding of a Hebrew University. Just before the cornerstone was laid, General Edmund Allenby, the British commander who had taken Jerusalem from the Turks on December 9, 1917, exclaimed, "We may be rolled back any minute! What is the good of beginning something you may never be able to finish?"

Weizmann answered, "This will be a great act of faith — faith in the victory which is bound to come, and faith in the future of Palestine!" On April 1, 1925, General Allenby was one of the guests from all over the world who attended the ceremony opening the Hebrew University in Jerusalem. Weizmann's great act of faith had been fulfilled.

Like Theodor Herzl, Weizmann believed that if you will it, and work hard enough for it, the Jewish state can happen. Like Herzl, he became the greatest leader of the Zionist movement, and was the head of the World Zionist Organization for many years, becoming its President in 1921.

Unlike Herzl, to whom Zionism came after he was 30, Weizmann became a Zionist at an early age. Until he was 11, he received only a Jewish education, learned how to write Hebrew, and collected money for Palestine. He was brought up in a small village and city, not in large world-famous cities, like Herzl. His parents had 15 children, 12 of whom lived, and eight of whom later settled in Palestine.

Chaim Weizmann was born in Motol, Russia, on November 17, 1874. His father, a timber merchant, was fond of books and learning, and the people of Motol often came to him to judge their disputes. Young Chaim listened and learned. After he was 11, he was sent to the city of Pinsk, 30 miles away, where he entered a Russian high school. His father was not wealthy, but he wanted his children to get the best possible education; eventually, nine of them went to a university.

Noticing how brilliant he was, Chaim's science teacher persuaded him to specialize in chemistry. The boy earned some money by giving private lessons. He received his board and lodging at the home of the owner of a chemical factory for teaching his two sons. Chaim himself took private Hebrew lessons. He received the highest grades in all subjects except drawing.

In 1892, he was ready to begin his higher education. Because Russian universities allowed only a small number of Jewish students to enter them, and because he thought that the sciences were taught better in Germany, Weizmann went to a polytechnic school in Darmstadt, Germany, and in 1893, enrolled in the Institute of Technology in Berlin to study biochemistry. In Berlin, Weizmann met other Russian Jews, with whom he discussed Zionism, Herzl's work, and *The Jewish State*.

Weizmann spent his vacations in Russia, where he urged Jewish people in the villages to support the Zionist movement. He was unable to get to the First Zionist Congress in 1897, but attended the next one in 1898 as a delegate, and others after that.

That same year, he studied at the University of Fribourg in Switzerland. He received the degree of Doctor of Philosophy in 1899. In 1901, he obtained a position in the University of Geneva. He made two industrial and chemical discoveries that he sold to large firms. Like Herzl, he could have followed a career that would have allowed him to live comfortably and possibly brought him wealth. However, also like Herzl, his ideal, the establishment of the Jewish national state, was more important to him than comfort and wealth.

Weizmann saw and heard Herzl at the Congresses that he attended. He and his friends were enthusiastic about Herzl's campaign at first, but they disagreed with his tactics of establishing a state overnight by dealing with rulers without first planning a process of education for the Jewish people.

However, they did not fight violently against Herzl. They formed a group to make their own views known. Weizmann especially urged cultural activities; he had begun to think about a Hebrew University while he was in Geneva.

At the Sixth Zionist Congress he was among those who voted against the Uganda offer. A famous story is told about Chaim Weizmann and the rejection of Uganda. About three years later, he met Lord Arthur James Balfour, then Prime Minister of Great Britain, who asked him why the British offer had been turned down.

Part of their conversation follows, with Dr. Weizmann first asking a question in return:

"Supposing I were to offer you Paris in place of London, would you take it?"

"But we already have London."

"When London was only a marsh, we already had Jerusalem, and we want to keep it."

Weizmann went from Switzerland to England and became a British citizen. He obtained a position in the University of Manchester, still keeping up his Zionist activities. He won over followers to Zionism and made the acquaintance of British officials, who praised his dignity and heroic quality.

Weizmann could be witty, companionable, and entertaining. He was above middle height but appeared to be taller, being powerfully built and of striking appearance. He had a dark mustache and a small pointed beard; his hair had begun to fall out when he was a young man, and he was almost completely bald by the time he was 40. With magnetic eyes and a kind of mystic strength, he possessed a charm and appeal now called charisma. Although not a spectacular speaker, he could dazzle an audience by his personality, wit, or a striking expression.

In 1906, he married Vera Chatzmann, whom he had met in Geneva, where she had come from Rostov, Russia, to study medicine, receiving her medical degree in 1906. The Weizmanns had two sons, Benjamin and Michael.

In 1938, at age 21, Michael, the younger son, joined the Royal Air Force. On February 11, 1942, he reported engine trouble while over the Bay of Biscay, and he and his plane disappeared. This tragedy weighed heavily on Chaim and Vera Weizmann for the rest of their lives. Winston Churchill often referred to the sacrifice made by Michael Weizmann for Great Britain.

When World War I broke out in 1914, Weizmann performed great services for his adopted country. He had become known for his work in industrial chemistry at the University and was called upon by the British Government to work in the field of explosives and fermentation.

Winston Churchill, then First Lord of the Admiralty, summoned Weizmann to London to manufacture a chemical needed for the naval guns. Churchill wanted 30,000 tons, and in a hurry. Dr. Weizmann answered that he had a very small quantity in his laboratory but that if he had a factory, he could make the amount needed. He got the factory, and Churchill got the 30,000 tons fast.

Weizmann met prominent officials, churchmen, writers, and members of the Rothschild family. To all of them he explained Zionist aims. C. P. Scott, editor of the *Manchester Guardian*, arranged a meeting with David Lloyd George, who later became Prime Minister, and Weizmann was introduced to Lord Balfour, Foreign Minister at that time.

At the same time, Zionists were also working in the United States and other countries to gain support for a Jewish state in Palestine.

Underground groups were fighting against the Turks and Germans in Palestine. Aaron Aaronsohn, a famous botanist and agronomist, or agricultural scientist, the discoverer of green wheat, from which sturdy species were developed, had organized a secret group in Palestine to aid the British Intelligence. His services were valuable to the British in the invasion of Palestine in 1917. He was now in London, seeing officials about the new state, and won a favorable hearing because of the great help given by his group, the Nili.

Weizmann called a number of Zionist meetings to draw up a document. After many revisions at these meetings and by British officials, this document was issued as a letter signed by Arthur James Balfour, dated November 1, 1917, and addressed to Lord Lionel Walter Rothschild. The full text follows; the part set off by quotation marks is the historic Balfour Declaration:

I have much pleasure in conveying to you, on behalf of His Majesty's Government, the following declaration of sympathy with Jewish Zionist aspirations which has been submitted to, and approved by, the Cabinet.

"His Majesty's Government view with favour the establishment in Palestine of a national home for the Jewish people, and will use their best endeavours to facilitate the achievement of this object, it being clearly understood that nothing shall be done which may prejudice the civil and religious rights of existing non-Jewish communities in Palestine, or the rights and political status enjoyed by Jews in any other country."

I should be grateful if you would bring this declaration to the knowledge of the Zionist Federation.

Lord Balfour was looked upon as a friend of the Jews and was an honored guest at the ceremony opening the Hebrew University in 1925. The allies of Great Britain endorsed the Balfour Declaration, and Jews all over the world rejoiced, for they thought that a Jewish state would be established in a very short time.

However, because of the opposition of many Arabs and changing policies of the British governments, it took more than 30 years until the new state arose. In 1918, Weizmann went to see Emir Feisal, a very powerful Arab leader, who did favor the creation of a Jewish state. Present at that meeting was Thomas E. Lawrence, better known as the famous Lawrence of Arabia. Feisal pledged his friendship, but other Arabs leaders forced him to give up any idea of cooperating with the Jews.

As allies of the Germans on the losing side in World War I, the Turks had to give up Palestine. The League of Nations assigned the rule over Palestine to Great Britain under a mandate, or commission, which

Chaim Weizmann

Lord Balfour

Henrietta Szold

lasted from 1922 to 1948. In 1929, the Jewish Agency was created to represent Jews throughout the world in dealings with the British. As leader of the World Zionist Organization, Dr. Weizmann headed the Agency from 1929 to 1931, and from 1935 to 1946.

During the period of the Mandate, the British Government issued a series of statements of policy called White Papers concerning Palestine. These appeared to favor the Arabs and to be hostile to the Jews. Weizmann was faced with a serious problem. He realized what harm the British policy was doing, but he was devoted to Great Britain and was sure that in the end she would help the Jews establish their state.

However, others in the Zionist movement did not feel that way. One group wanted immediate action, revolt, if necessary, against the British in Palestine. Another group wanted a different kind of control of the Zionist organization, a shift to socialistic thought. There were bitter struggles throughout the years, not only at the Congresses but in different countries, like England, the United States, and also Palestine. Finally, in July, 1931, the opposition was so strong that Weizmann was voted out of office at the 17th Zionist Congress meeting in Basle.

Once more he devoted himself to science, did research in organic chemistry and biochemistry, and wrote articles for scientific journals. He also became director of the Daniel Sieff Research Institute in Rehovoth, which he dedicated on April 3, 1939, as a memorial to Michael Weizmann's young friend, who had met a tragic death in Palestine. With the consent of the Sieff family, who had given the funds to have it built, the Daniel Sieff Research Institute was later made part of the Weizmann Research Institute.

On this visit to Rehovoth with Dr. Weizmann, his wife saw a spot with a beautiful view and suggested that they buy the land. A few years later, they had a home built there which was called the Weizmann House, in which they lived whenever they were in Palestine. It is now like a national shrine.

Although Weizmann was no longer the head of the World Zionist Organization, he continued to work for Zionism. He was still head of the English Zionist Federation, and he worked to get the Jews out of Germany and settle them in Palestine as Hitler came into power. He was President of the Youth Aliyah, which sent Jewish children to Palestine from Germany and other countries.

In Palestine, the children brought in by the Youth Aliyah were taken care of by a heroine of Israel, Miss Henrietta Szold (1860-1945), an American who had settled in Palestine at age 60. She had been President of the Daughters of Zion, which later changed its name to Hadassah, the famous Women's Zionist Organization of America. She came to Palestine in 1920 to organize nursing schools, child-care centers, dispensaries, and hospitals.

Weizmann traveled to many countries to raise funds for the Keren Hayesod, the Foundation Fund, which he had helped found in London for all activities in Palestine except the buying of land. He made a memorable trip to South Africa, visited Germany, and appeared at the 1933 World's Fair in Chicago where he was given a fee of $100,000. This he donated to the relief of German Jews. He made other trips to the United States. Each time he was greeted by enormous, enthusiastic crowds.

As the greatest Jew in public life, he was asked in 1935 to become again the President of the World Zionist Organization. He faced a critical situation after World War II ended in 1945. During the war, the Jews had supported Great Britain against the Nazis in spite of her policy.

Now, as Arabs attacks were multiplying, and British troops were clashing with the Jews, there was open hostility. Some groups called for greater resistance, guerrilla warfare, and reprisals against the British as well as against the Arabs. Others were resorting to terrorism, which Weizmann and other leaders opposed. He himself advised patience, still believing that in the end Great Britain would act in favor of the Jews.

Under these circumstances, the 22nd Zionist Congress met in Basle in December, 1946. When Weizmann urged "peaceful beliefs," saying, "The Jewish people had come to Palestine to build and not to destroy," a delegate shouted "Demagogue" at him. Weizmann remained firm and in his closing speech he declared, "Zion shall be redeemed in Judgement! — and not by any other means." However, opposition to a peaceful policy continued.

A few days later, a motion that Weizmann favored was defeated, and he resigned as President. He returned to Rehovoth, where he engaged in scientific work and watched the growth of the Weizmann Institute of Science.

Meanwhile, he met with prominent leaders of other countries who were members of the United Nations Special Committee on Palestine. In October, 1947, he and Mrs. Weizmann went to New York where he appeared before a Committee of the United Nations. He consulted with President Harry S. Truman, who promised support for the formation of the new state. After the United Nations had passed the resolution on November 29, 1947 for the partition of Palestine, giving part of it to the Jews, Weizmann, now 73, was thoroughly exhausted and ill and decided to go home via London, India, and Burma.

However, in London, urgent calls came from New York asking him to return to the United States at once. Moshe Sharett, member of the

Executive Committee of the Jewish Agency, telephoned; Abba Eban, later Ambassador to the United States, Permanent Delegate to the United Nations, and Foreign Minister of Israel, sent a cable.

Weizmann's diplomatic ability and appeal were needed. Great Britain and the United States were hesitating about putting the partition plan into effect.

Weizmann and his wife arrived in New York on February 4, 1948 during a blizzard. He became ill, a victim of influenza. In spite of his illness, he corresponded and made telephone calls. He arose from a sickbed to go to Washington to see President Truman, who promised that he would recognize the Jewish state. Later, he said that Weizmann was the only man who could have sold him the idea. Truman praised Weizmann highly, calling him "a very great man...of remarkable achievements and personality."

Weizmann got a message through to David Ben-Gurion, head of the Palestinian Jews, urging that the state be declared at once. On May 14, 1948, a few hours before the British gave up their Mandate, the world was thrilled by the news from Tel Aviv that Israel had come into existence.

All this time, Chaim Weizmann was in a sickbed, physically unable to enjoy to the full the moment of his greatest triumph. On the 16th of May, Ben-Gurion and four other leaders sent him a cable in which they referred to him as the one who had done more than any other living man toward the creation of the Jewish state. Then came the news that Chaim Weizmann had been chosen President of the Provisional Government of Israel.

He became President after the first national election in 1949, and again in 1951. He suffered a few heart attacks and died on November 9, 1952, at age 78. As he had requested, he was buried on his own grounds at Rehovoth. The Weizmann Institute of Science, which has expanded enormously since it was opened about 20 years ago and has become a great institution of scientific education and research, is a memorial to him. A greater memorial is his part in the building of Israel.

A great and heroic man, according to Sir Isaiah Berlin of Oxford University, a faithful friend and follower of Chaim Weizmann, may be one who helps bring about a change for the better that deeply and permanently alters human lives. By taking an active part in that change, he makes that which seems highly improbable, or even miraculous, happen.

Dr. Chaim Weizmann was that type of great and heroic man. He expressed part of Sir Isaiah Berlin's idea more briefly in these words, which apply to his own work in bringing about the creation of the State of Israel:

"Difficult things take a long time, the impossible takes a little longer."

Amphitheatre of the old University of Jerusalem on Mount Scopus

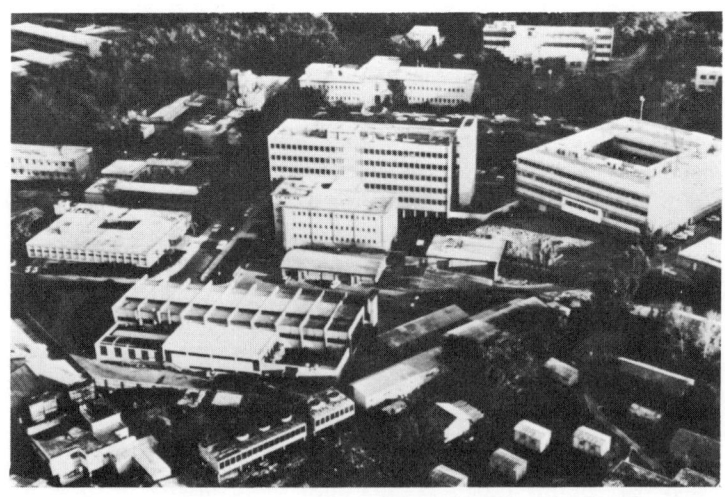

Weizmann Institute

4

David Ben-Gurion

Pioneer to Prime Minister

Zionism's third great leader was David Ben-Gurion, a man almost totally different from Theodor Herzl and Chaim Weizmann. He was a pioneer who came to Palestine to work as a farmer, and a man dedicated to the interests of workers. He changed his last name from *Green* to a Hebrew name, *Ben-Gurion.*

David was born in Plonsk, Poland, then part of Russia, on October, 16, 1886, the sixth of 11 children born to Avigdor and Sheindal Green. His father was a learned and progressive man who spoke Hebrew and was a Zionist.

Avigdor and his friends used to meet at his home to discuss Zionism, and young David soon had the desire to speak Hebrew and become a Zionist himself. At 14, he, one of his brothers, and a few friends, formed a Zionist society. The members collected funds for the Zionist movement, studied and discussed politics and history.

They also thought about the injustices in Czarist Russia, especially toward the Jews. Like some of their elders, these serious-minded youths thought that the growing Socialist movement would do away with poverty. They believed that if they ever reached Palestine, they would build a nation in which social injustices did not exist. David joined a society called *Poale Zion*, "Workers of Zion," formed by Socialist Zionists.

In 1904, David went to Warsaw to study. Because he was active in organizing labor and in Zionist affairs, the police pounced on him as a "trouble-maker," and he spent a day in jail.

Shlomo Zemach, a very close friend of David, had gone to Palestine. In 1906, he came home for a brief visit. When the time came for him to go back to Palestine, David and a few of the townspeople of Plonsk went with him. Arriving at the port of Jaffa, David was so eager to get to a Jewish village that he did not spend a single night there. Accompanied by Shlomo, he set out on foot soon after arrival for Petah Tikvah ("Gate of Hope"), called "the mother of Jewish settlements."

David was so overjoyed with being in the Land of Israel that he lay awake all night listening to the sounds of the animals on the farm and in the fields and to the murmuring of the distant sea. He looked out upon skies and stars that he had never seen. He was overcome by happiness; the spirit and dreams of his youth had triumphed. One thought ran through his mind, "The Land of Israel is here, wherever I turn or tread."

David Ben-Gurion kept this love of the land, this closeness between himself and nature all his life.

At the beginning, he and Shlomo faced difficulties. They had to

David Ben-Gurion

work for small wages because the farmers employed Arabs who were paid very little. The work was hard, and David grew weak because he could not buy enough food. Finally, he contracted malaria.

Objecting to the policy of the "gentlemen-farmers," as he called them, David, again with Shlomo, left for Rishon Le Zion, where they worked in the wine cellars. Then came a short stay in a new settlement, Kfar Saba, where David began to study Arabic, which he learned to speak well.

In the same year, 1907, he was again on the move. He trudged 60 miles to Sejera, a pioneer village in Galilee, where he finally found what he was looking for in Palestine. As he wrote to his father, here he felt that he had come home. Entire families, the men, women, and children, were doing all the work on the land.

At Sejera, Ben-Gurion received his first military training. A woman named Manya Wilbushevitz, who later married a settler named Israel Shochat, organized a defense group called Bar Giora, after one of the leaders in the siege of Jerusalem by Titus. The name was soon changed to *Hashomer*, "The Guard" ("Watchmen"). Such units were also formed in other settlements, and from Hashomer grew the famous Haganah, the Jewish underground army in Palestine, later the basis of the regular army.

Ben-Gurion and another settler, Itzhak Ben-Zvi, played an important part in Hashomer at Sejera, fighting against Arab raiders. The two men had met earlier at a Zionist Conference in Jaffa, became good friends, and worked together for a long time. Later, Ben-Zvi gave up political activities to devote himself to scholarship and writing, but in 1952, Ben-Gurion called upon him to serve his country again — this time as the second President of Israel.

Ben-Zvi was called from Sejera to join the Workers of Zion in Jerusalem. A few months later, he sent an urgent message to Ben-Gurion to come at once because his talents as an organizer and his knowledge of Hebrew were needed. Ben-Zvi had been asked to set up a Hebrew publication called *Achdut*, "Unity." Ben-Gurion felt that his place was on a farm because he had come to Palestine to work on the soil. However Ben-Zvi convinced him that the work in Jerusalem was just as important, and Ben-Gurion became an editor of *Unity*.

This was when he changed his last name, *Green*, to *Ben-Gurion*. Many Palestinian Jews were changing their last names and even their first names to Hebrew ones to feel that they were home in their own land.

Ben-Gurion wrote articles and made speeches. He pleaded for the unity of all Jews, for the use of Hebrew as an everyday language, and for the acceptance of the socialistic ideals of the Workers of Zion. For his work as an editor, writer, and speaker, he received about $2.25 a week. Still, he found the work enjoyable and rewarding. No matter how high a position he held later, he loved to refer to himself as a journalist.

In 1913, he went to Constantinople to study Turkish law in the Ottoman University School of Law. There had been a revolution in the Turkish, or Ottoman, Empire. The Palestinian Jews thought the new government would become more liberal — that some day Jews would sit in the Turkish Parliament. Therefore, Ben-Gurion, followed by Ben-Zvi, Moshe Shertok, who later changed his name to Sharett, and a few others, felt that a knowledge of Turkish law would be most useful. Incidentally, Moshe Sharett later held many important positions in Palestine and Israel, and was Prime Minister from 1953 to 1955. Ever a student of languages, Ben-Gurion learned Turkish in Constantinople.

When World War I broke out in 1914, Ben-Gurion and Ben-Zvi were in Palestine. Shertok had been taken into the Turkish army as an officer. Ben-Gurion and Ben-Zvi were arrested, charged with conspiring to form a Jewish state, and were deported to Alexandria, Egypt, at that time under British control. The British looked upon them as enemy aliens but finally allowed them to leave for the United States in 1915.

There, Ben-Gurion learned another language, English. He and Ben-Zvi went from state to state, pleading the cause of Zionism. They wrote books, lectured, and recruited pioneers. In New York, Ben-Gurion met Paula Munweiss, a student nurse. They were married in 1917.

In London, Vladimir Ze'ev Jabotinsky, whom Ben-Gurion had met in Constantinople, had, after many efforts, persuaded the British to form a Jewish Legion. Ben-Gurion and Ben-Zvi worked to gain recruits in the United States. They themselves enlisted, and after a course of training in Canada, landed in Egypt in August, 1918. Ben-Gurion was made a corporal, but became ill with dysentery and had to spend a long time in a hospital. While there, he received word that his wife, who had remained in New York, had given birth to their first child, a daughter named Geula, "Redemption."

After the war ended, Ben-Gurion met two men who had a great influence on him. One of them, Berl Katznelson, became his dearest friend. He was of about the same age as Ben-Gurion, had come from Russia three years after him, and was a founder of the colony of Kinneret. He had the same social and labor views as Ben-Gurion, had also worked to organize a Jewish fighting force, and joined the Jewish Legion. Katznelson was a learned man who was known as "The Teacher." He had once been a teacher and librarian.

The other friend was Eliahu Golomb, a few years younger than Ben-Gurion. He stressed the need of a Jewish military organization and helped form a group of volunteers to aid the British when General Allenby's army captured Jerusalem in December, 1917. Ben-Gurion saw in Golomb the Israeli of the future, a man who combined military and intellectual ability. Golomb began the organization of *Haganah*, "Defense," and was supported by Ben-Gurion, Ben-Zvi, and Katznelson.

When Ben-Gurion's wife, Paula, and their daughter, Geula, returned from New York, the family lived in Tel Aviv. However, public duties called Ben-Gurion away from home life. Under the guidance of Katznelson, he formed a political party called *Achdut Avoda*, "Unity of Labor," which sent him as a delegate to an important Zionist Conference held in London in July, 1920. His wife and daughter joined him there a little later.

In London, the second child of the Ben-Gurions was born, a boy they named Amos. Ben-Gurion, who never gave up his love of working in the fields, chose the name of this prophet because he had been a herdsman of sheep and goats. The Ben-Gurions' third child, a daughter, Renana, "Rejoicing," was born in Palestine in 1929, the only sabra, or native-born, in the family.

At the London Conference, Ben-Gurion and Weizmann clashed for the first time. Weizmann was the acknowledged leader of the Zionist movement; Ben-Gurion, 12 years younger than Weizmann, was unknown internationally, and represented only about 2,000 members of a labor group in Palestine.

The two men were unlike in appearance, background, education, social life and views. Weizmann was taller, dignified looking, a university graduate, and a famous scientist. Ben-Gurion was short and stocky, mostly self-educated, interested in languages rather than in science, and identified with socialism and the workingman. Weizmann believed in moving slowly. Ben-Gurion wanted more aggressive leadership and quicker action.

On his return to Palestine, Ben-Gurion became one of the organizers of *Histadrut*, the General Federation of Jewish Labor, and was elected its Secretary-General. Today, it represents more than 90% of all the workers in Israel and includes Arabs as well as Jews.

In 1920, the British were in charge of maintaining order in Palestine and used Arab police as assistants. Hadj Amin El Husseini came forward as an important leader. Some landowners who had sold land to the Jews at high prices now wanted the land back because it had been improved. (Hadj Amin later became the Grand Mufti of Jerusalem; a mufti is a judge of religious law.)

A mob was stirred up and attacked the Jews in Jerusalem as the Arab police looked on. Some Jews were killed, and a great many were wounded. The Jews organized defense units; among their leaders was Vladimir Jabotinsky. The British arrested him and more than 20 of his followers and put them in prison. Hadj Amin fled, but some Arabs were arrested and jailed.

Sir Herbert Samuel, a Jew, was appointed the first High Commissioner under the British Mandate. Not wanting to be accused of being pro-Jewish, he pardoned all the prisoners, Arabs as well as Jews, the attackers and the attacked. Meanwhile, massacres of Jews took place in a number of settlements.

In 1929, when Sir Herbert Samuel was no longer the Commissioner, a great massacre took place in many parts of Palestine. The British officials had been warned, but they did nothing to prevent or stop the killings. They held a court of inquiry, but instead of seeking out and punishing the assassins, the British issued the White Paper of 1930 limiting immigration and the purchase of land.

In that year, working to reach his favorite goal of unity, Ben-Gurion consulted with Katznelson and other leaders of labor groups. They reached an agreement out of which grew the Mapai, the United Workers Party, which became the most powerful political party in Israel.

After Adolf Hitler was elected Chancellor of Germany on January 30, 1933, the Zionists worked to get as many Jews as they could out of Germany. In the next three years at least 150,000 Jews entered Palestine in a great Aliyah. This large number infuriated the Grand Mufti. Ben-Gurion made several attempts to reach him and come to terms with the Arabs, but failed.

Ben-Gurion was now the leader of the Jews in Palestine and one of the recognized leaders of the Zionist movement. In 1933, he had so many followers that he gained control of the Zionist Congress and was chosen to be a member of the Executive (like a Cabinet) of the Jewish Agency and the World Zionist Organization. Two years later, he became chairman.

Many troubled years lay ahead that required the utmost firmness, courage, and ability to face the most trying opposition. Ben-Gurion had to withstand the attacks of the Arabs, fight against the policy of the British Government, and meet the opposition of Jewish leaders who wanted things done differently.

In April, 1936, under orders of the Grand Mufti, the Arabs once more made a massive attack upon the Jews. He also organized attacks upon the British and even Arabs who did not agree with him. At last, the British took action, ordering his arrest, but he escaped. He appeared later in other parts of Asia and in Europe, preaching hatred of the Jews and speaking against the British and in favor of the Germans.

The British Government sent a commission under Lord William Robert Peel to Palestine to bring back recommendations for ending the dispute between the Arabs and the Jews. The Peel Report of 1937 did not bring peace but increased hostility and division. The Report recommended that Great Britain should retain control of part of Palestine, including Jerusalem, and that the rest should be split up between the Arabs and Jews, with the Jews receiving only a tiny portion.

The Arabs rejected this plan; the Jews were divided. The Revisionists, a group led by Jabotinsky, wanted all of Biblical Palestine; almost all the Histadrut leaders were against the plan. Weizmann was willing to give it a trial. Ben-Gurion felt that small as the territory offered was, it was better for the Jews to have their own state at last, and that living in a free state of their own was better than living under a mandate. The plan was never tried out, for the British themselves kept postponing action on it.

They were still limiting immigration for fear of antagonizing the Arabs. An order was issued that over the next five years only 15,000 Jews were to be admitted yearly, and the British Government promised that some day Palestine would be made an independent Arab state. The official name of this order was the Palestine White Paper, and it became the most hateful of all the White Papers. Ben-Gurion is said to have told Lord Edward Halifax, the British Foreign Secretary, "You will not enforce it, except with bayonets."

Soon after the publication of the White Paper, World War II broke out. Although the Arabs were generally hostile to them, the British did not soften their policy toward the Jews, whose help they would now need in Palestine. The Zionists were faced with a problem. To support the Germans was unthinkable because, if the Germans won, there would be no hope for the Jews, least of all for a Jewish state. If Great Britain and her Allies won, there was a chance that she might change her policy. Therefore, Great Britain had to be supported, but its plan for Palestine had to be opposed. Ben-Gurion then uttered the famous words that became the slogan and policy of the Zionists, "We will fight the war as if there were no White Paper, and the White Paper as if there were no war."

Dr. Weizmann and Ben-Gurion, then in England, tried to get British officials to form a Jewish Brigade to fight on their side. Ben-Gurion was advised to go to the United States, which was not yet in the war, to talk about the Nazi danger. While he was there, the Japanese made the attack on Pearl Harbor on December 7, 1941, which brought the United States into the war.

On April 11, 1942, an emergency conference of Zionist delegates from all over the world met at the Hotel Biltmore, New York. Ben-Gurion proposed what came to be called the Biltmore Program or Resolution: a Jewish army had to be formed; immigration should be unlimited; all of Palestine must become a Jewish commonwealth. The Biltmore Program would mean the end of the White Paper.

About five months after the Biltmore meeting, Prime Minister Churchill, who was friendly to Zionism, announced that the British Government would allow the formation of a Jewish Brigade to fight under a Star of David flag and wear a Star of David shoulder patch. The Brigade fought valiantly in Egypt and Italy and was among the victorious troops entering Berlin.

When the war ended in 1945, the Jews thought that their dream of a state would now come true. They had helped the British, while the Arabs had stood aside or helped the Germans. Moreover, the British Government was now Labor, but Ernest Bevin, the new Foreign Secretary, proved to be no friend of the Jews. He supported the White Paper and did not wish to antagonize the Arabs.

Ben-Gurion and other Jewish leaders had to engage in political and diplomatic maneuvers at the United Nations and in the capitals of foreign countries to get the British to change their policy and to win support for a Jewish state. At home, he faced serious problems brought on by armed groups that decided they had had enough of slow tactics and negotiations.

The *Irgun Zvai Leumi*, "National Military Organization," formed in 1937, believed in striking back, unlike the Haganah. Among their early leaders were David Raziel (killed while fighting for the British in World War II) and Vladimir Jabotinsky (died in 1940). In 1944, Menahem Begin (Beigin) became their leader. A more violent group, the *Lehi*, "Fighters for the Freedom of Israel," had broken away from the Irgun. They are often called the Stern Gang, after their leader, Abraham Stern.

The Stern Gang attacked both British and Arabs. They bombed buildings, took vengeance upon Arab terrorists by acts of terrorism, like the massacre of villagers at Deir Yassin, assassinated a British official, and captured British soldiers whom they tried and executed. The British authorities replied with fierce tactics. The actions of the Stern Gang brought great distress to Ben-Gurion and other leaders who did not believe in terrorism.

All the groups helped to get immigrants into Palestine in defiance of the British ban or limitations. They were brought in secretly, smuggled over borders, transported in old ships, many of which were caught by the British and turned back. Some of the ships sank or exploded with great loss of life.

It was during this period that the famous voyage of *Exodus 1947* was made, when the British would not allow this ship carrying refugees

Exodus 1947

Declaration of the State of Israel

formerly held in German concentration camps to enter Palestine. The entire story of the "illegal" immigration into Palestine is a tragic and heroic epic.

A state of war existed in Palestine. Bevin sent troops and accused the Jewish leaders of revolting. In 1946, the British rounded up as many of them as they could and placed them in jail. Among them were some who had fought on their side, like Moshe Sharett and Itzhak Rabin. Fortunately, Ben-Gurion, who was in London at that time, was able to find safety in Paris.

The harsh actions taken by the British did not end Jewish resistance. Realizing that Great Britain alone could not solve the problem, Bevin freed the prisoners and tried to arrange a meeting between Arab and Jewish leaders in London, but the Arabs refused to meet with the Jews.

As a final way out, Bevin put the matter before the United Nations, which decided on November 29, 1947 that Britain would leave Palestine by August 1, 1948, and that two months later Palestine would be divided into Arab and Jewish states, with Bethlehem and Jerusalem under international control. Great Britain announced that it would leave on May 15.

About six months were left in which to organize the new state. The 600,000 Jews in Palestine were without a government, and the British did nothing to help them take over. The Arab world of more than 40,000,000 was hostile. Raids were being made upon the Jewish sections, and forces of the Arab states surrounding the coming state were waiting beyond the border, ready to attack when the British left.

Such were the conditions facing Ben-Gurion and the Jewish people. They were outnumbered, ill-armed, and ill-equipped, but they had the will and determination to fight to the end. "We have no alternative," they would say.

As the British left, they turned over to the Arabs some of the fortified places and stores of ammunition. British officers were training Arab troops. As head of the Jewish Agency, Ben-Gurion was the leader of the people and rallied them to resist.

Representatives of Jewish organizations met in a museum building in Tel Aviv on May 14, 1948. After the Israel Philharmonic Orchestra played *Hatikvah,* "The Hope," which became the national anthem, Ben-Gurion read the Proclamation, or Declaration, of Independence, and the State of Israel was born. A provisional, or temporary, government was formed, with Ben-Gurion as Prime Minister, or Premier, and Defense Minister.

Troops from Egypt, Iraq, Jordan, Lebanon, Saudi Arabia, and Syria rushed across the frontiers. Ben-Gurion conferred with military leaders and directed the defense. Supplies and ammunition arrived from abroad before Egyptian ships could prevent cargo vessels from bringing them in.

The Israelis, as the citizens of the new state are called, beat the Arabs on all fronts, except near Jerusalem. In defiance of the United Nations partition plan, the Arabs had occupied the Old City, but they failed to take the New City. Alarmed at the situation, the United Nations sent Count Folke Bernadotte of Sweden to arrange a truce. The two sides accepted a one-month cease-fire beginning on June 11, 1948. Neither side was to import war supplies. However, the Irgun had already arranged to have an arms shipment brought in on the steamer *Altalena*, which arrived three days after the cease-fire went into effect.

Ben-Gurion was faced with a serious problem. The Irgun had acted on its own, but the ammunition was badly needed, and Menahem Begin, the Irgun leader, had agreed to share it with the other troops. If Ben-Gurion accepted it, he would be breaking his word to Count Bernadotte and prove to the outside world that he was not in control. He therefore ordered Begin to radio the ship not to come into port. Defying this command, Begin went to Tel Aviv harbor, rowed to the ship, and directed it to a landing place. With the consent of a majority of the Cabinet, Ben-Gurion ordered shore-batteries to fire upon the *Altalena*, which burst into flames. Almost 100 men were killed or wounded. Many of the Irgun jumped from the ship. Some, including Begin, escaped, others were arrested.

It had been a hard decision for Ben-Gurion. To maintain order and authority he had ordered fellow-Israelis to be fired upon. Moreover, the ammunition was going to be needed since the Arabs were sure to attack again. However, most of his countrymen agreed that Ben-Gurion had done the right thing.

When the truce ended, the Arabs attacked and were beaten again. Count Bernadotte was working on a peace plan, which, it was said, was making changes in the partition plan and would give Jerusalem to the Arabs. He was assassinated in Jerusalem on September 17, 1948.

About 300 of the Stern Gang were arrested. Other terrorists were rounded up, or they voluntarily disbanded or promised to give up all terrorist activity. Two leaders of the Stern Gang were tried for the murder of Count Bernadotte, but there was not enough evidence against them. The murderers were never caught.

Dr. Ralph Bunche of the United States took Count Bernadotte's place as the United Nations mediator. He succeeded in getting Egypt and Israel to sign an armistice agreement on the island of Rhodes, Greece, on February, 24, 1949. At later intervals that year, Lebanon, Jordan, and Syria also signed agreements, but Iraq refused. In spite of the agreements, there has been a state of war ever since, sometimes breaking out in full-scale wars, as in 1956 and 1967, and the tempo of fighting has increased since 1968. Moreover, the Arab nations have never recognized the existence of Israel as a nation, and there are no commercial or diplomatic relations between Israel and the Arab world.

In 1949, after the first elections held in Israel, Ben-Gurion became the Prime Minister, or Premier, and was named to that post again after the following election in 1951. The Premier there is the head of the government; the President has very little power.

After Israel became an independent state, a regular army was organized. It took in the fighting units like Haganah and Palmach, its elite corps. The name of the unified fighting forces is *Zahal*, the Israel Defense Forces (IDF), which includes the naval and air forces. The Minister of Defense is the Commander in Chief.

Great numbers of Jewish immigrants arrived and were freely admitted in accordance with the Israeli Declaration of Independence, which guarantees that the State of Israel will be open for Jewish immigration and the "ingathering of the exiles" from all the countries of their dispersion.

One of the most dramatic of these "ingatherings" was called Operation Magic Carpet. Since the destruction of the First Temple, Jews had been living in Yemen, a small country along the Red Sea south of Saudi Arabia. After the State of Israel was born, Yemenite Jews flocked to Aden, a city under British control south of Yemen.

With the help of the Joint Distribution Committee of American Jews, chartered planes transported the entire number, about 50,000, carrying about 140 in each plane at least five times a day. This was Operation Magic Carpet, but to the Yemenites, who knew the Bible well, the planes were "eagles' wings." Getting into the planes they thought of the prophecy of Isaiah, "They that wait upon the Lord...shall mount up with wings as eagles," and on arriving in Israel, they recalled the words of Exodus, " I bore you on eagles' wings and brought you to myself."

Israel is the only true democracy in the Middle East; the large number of political parties and often bitter debates in the Knesset ("Assembly," "Council"), or Parliament, exist because there is an opportunity for all shades of opinion to be represented and expressed. Menahem Begin, former head of Irgun, is a member; there are also a few Arab representatives.

In 1953, Ben-Gurion resigned as Premier and was succeeded by Moshe Sharett. Ben-Gurion was 66, had been active in political life for almost 50 years, and felt he needed a rest. Under his leadership, the country had made a good beginning and was prospering. New settlements were founded, schools, homes, and factories were being built, art, music, and the theater were flourishing.

Together with his wife, Paula, he went to live in Sde Boker, "Field of the Herdsman," a small kibbutz in the Negev. He had long urged the development of the Negev, and, as when he named his son *Amos*, he was attracted by anything that had to do with herdsmen.

Ben-Gurion chose to live in a kibbutz because he felt that Israel needed more of the pioneering spirit that the early settlers like himself had brought to the land about 50 years before. He longed for a return to the soil, for he really did not care for life in big cities.

A kibbutz is a settlement in which the members own everything in common and a committee decides policy. Ben-Gurion did not go to Sde Boker as a privileged character, but he and his wife shared work with the others, most of them young. He has never felt "the generation gap." The only concession made to him and his wife was that they were given a three-room hut, but they ate meals in the common dining hall.

He worked as a shepherd, cleaned the cattle-stalls, and wheeled barrels of fodder. After his morning's work, Ben-Gurion read, studied, or wrote letters and articles, for he still considered himself a journalist. He read from the works of Greek authors, like the historian Thucydides and the philosopher Plato, in the original language, which he had begun to study many years before.

Sometimes, distinguished visitors came to see Ben-Gurion and his wife. He did not leave Sde Boker to attend meetings except when asked by the Minister of Education to address youth groups. For them he had a constant message, that the future of Israel depended on their settling in new villages near the frontiers. The struggle with the enemy was not yet over, and the borders had to be guarded.

Ben-Gurion spoke truly, for in 1954 the situation was becoming very serious. King Farouk of Egypt had been overthrown by a military revolt led by Lieutenant Colonel Gamal Abdel Nasser, an old foe of Israel, who became Premier of Egypt, now a republic. Arab guerrilla bands were being formed; Nasser boasted that the Arabs would crush the Zionists. At the urgent request of Prime Minister Moshe Sharett, Ben-Gurion returned to Jerusalem in February, 1955, and became the Minister of Defense. He warned the Egyptians that Israel would not tolerate raids against its territory.

After the general election of July, 1955, President Ben-Zvi asked

Ben-Gurion to form a new government. Sharett willingly gave up his position as Prime Minister and resumed his former post as Foreign Minister, while Ben-Gurion once more became both Prime Minister and Minister of Defense.

In June 1956, Colonel Nasser was elected President of Egypt, and a month later his government took the Suez Canal and seized control of the Suez Canal Company's property, which had been owned mainly by the French and English. Nasser was receiving weapons from the Russians, who were now aiding the Arabs in order that they themselves might obtain the greatest influence in the Middle East. So, Russia, one of the first two nations to recognize Israel, turned against her and has been more hostile ever since.

Nasser threatened to attack Israel at any moment. He closed the Gulf of Aqaba and the Straits of Tiran to Israeli ships, an act of war, and had himself made commander of the united armies of Egypt, Jordan, and Syria. Israel struck back on October 29, 1956, and quickly overwhelmed the Egyptians. When Nasser refused to agree to a cease-fire requested by the French and British, they went into action and occupied Port Said, Ismailia, and Suez. Both the French and British were angered at Nasser for taking over the Suez Canal Company.

Russia and the United States now stepped in. Prime Minister Bulganin of the Soviet Union and President Dwight D. Eisenhower sent letters to Ben-Gurion advising Israel to give up her conquests. Pressure was also put on Great Britain and France to withdraw from Egypt. The United Nations, of course, had called for a cease-fire.

Russia was trying to save Nasser and might use military force, if Israel refused to leave the conquered territory. Israel might also lose the goodwill and future help of the United States. Once more, Ben-Gurion had to make a painful decision. He recalled the Israeli troops from the occupied areas after he had declared to the Knesset and the people that they would stay there until Nasser signed peace terms.

On one point Israel did not yield without guarantees. She did not immediately give up the Gaza Strip and the land along the Gulf of Aqaba that the Egyptians had been using as a base from which to fire upon Israeli ships. Incidentally, the Gaza Strip had not been given to Egypt in the original partition plan. Finally, the United Nations guaranteed freedom of shipping to Israel and stationed observers to safeguard the Gaza Strip and the Sinai area.

However, in spite of the guarantees, Egypt still did not allow Israel to use the Suez Canal. Moreover, Nasser's request to the United Nations to recall the observers in 1967 (which was granted) and his renewed

Ben-Gurion and fellow workers, Sde Boker

closing of the Straits of Tiran and the Gulf of Aqaba to Israeli ships were among the causes of the war in June, 1967.

Ben-Gurion was out of office from 1959 to 1960. He made a brief visit to the United States to receive an honorary degree of Doctor of Laws from Brandeis University. In 1963, Ben-Gurion retired at age 77 and went again to Sde Boker. Still stocky and sturdy, he had only a thin fringe of hair, which had turned white years before.

In 1967, Ben-Gurion made another trip to the United States to raise funds for Israel; he was greeted with the same enthusiasm as in 1951 when he took part in the first sale of State of Israel bonds.

His beloved wife, Paula, died in 1968. She had been his most devoted helper and greatest supporter. From the day she first met him in 1917, she felt "he was a great man." She declared then, "I could tell that he was like one of the prophets out of the Bible."

Many others who lived through the events of his time also feel that he is like a figure out of the Bible that he knows so well. Which one is a matter of choice and opinion. Both he and Israel are physically small, but immense in their deeds. Like his namesake, David, they have had to fight against a giant.

The story of David Ben-Gurion and modern Israel are interwoven. In his life-story you have read about almost the entire history of Israel for more than 50 years, from its pioneering days, its struggles to become a nation, its growth and triumphs until its present fight for survival. In that period of half a century, a strong hand and keen mind were needed to give guidance. They were found in David Ben-Gurion.

Itzhak Ben-Zvi   Moshe Sharett

5

Joseph Trumpeldor
"Never Mind."

"If I should be killed in battle, I die for the Jewish people, for our ideals." These words were written by Joseph Trumpeldor when he was fighting against the Turks in World War I. Never running from danger, never fearing death, he became the first military hero of the Jewish settlers in Palestine.

Joseph Trumpeldor was born in Piatagorsk, Russia, in 1880. Ever since he was a boy, he met with anti-Semitism, read about Zionism, and became a devoted Zionist. After studying dentistry, he was called to military duty in 1902. As an educated person, he could have done office work in the army but insisted on doing everything the other privates had to do. He looked upon all work as honorable and did not want the other soldiers to think that, as a Jew, he was shirking his duties.

Trumpeldor organized Zionist groups among the Jewish soldiers. In 1904, war broke out between Russia and Japan. His regiment was sent to Port Arthur, Manchuria. Once more, Trumpeldor could have avoided front-line duty. His commanding officer, needing office help, wanted him to be made a warrant (subordinate, noncommissioned) officer. Trumpeldor won his request to be sent to the front.

In a letter to his family, he explained his action. Most Russians thought that the Jews were cowardly and disloyal, and he wanted to prove that they could be as brave and loyal as any other Russian. Trumpeldor fought so well that he was promoted to the rank of sergeant and assigned to a special unit that engaged in very dangerous missions.

An incident took place which shows what Trumpeldor and other Jews had to face in Russia and elsewhere. While lecturing the men on the nature of their work, an officer of the unit said he hoped that there were no cowards or deserters among them, because not one of them was a Jew. Trumpeldor bravely walked out of the ranks, stood at attention, and proudly declared, "I do not consider myself a coward or a deserter, and I am a Jew."

Trumpeldor was tall, handsome, with a deep chest, broad shoulders, a long pleasant face, and bold, penetrating eyes. The officer looked at him with amazement but said nothing in front of the men. Later, he told Trumpeldor that he had not meant to offend him. The officer gave the same explanation so often given by others like him — that Trumpeldor was not like the other Jews.

Trumpeldor showed such bravery and leadership that he was

Joseph Trumpeldor

awarded the Cross of St. George, the highest decoration in Czarist Russia. On August 7, 1904, he was hit by a shell in the left arm which had to be amputated almost to the shoulder. He did not groan but smiled and said, "Never mind. The right hand is more useful." Expressed in different ways, "Never mind," became the slogan of his life.

He was discharged from the army after three months in a hospital but asked to remain in service. He was willing to fight with a sword and revolver, but no private or noncommissioned officer could serve without a rifle. However, because of Trumpeldor's record and bravery, the commanding officer of the regiment made an exception for him and even ordered that a special medal should be awarded to him.

Port Arthur was captured by the Japanese, and Trumpeldor was among the men taken prisoner and sent to a camp in Japan. There, he organized classes in Zionism among the Jewish prisoners. He formed a small group that promised to go to Palestine as soon as they could. In spite of all his efforts to become a Jewish hero among the Russians, the officers considered him and the other Jews as second-class citizens. Even in the prison camp, they arranged that Russians and Jews should have separate living quarters. Trumpeldor realized that Russia could never be his true home when he returned to it.

After the signing of a peace treaty between Russia and Japan, Trumpeldor returned home early in 1906. He was given more medals, called a great hero, and made an officer in the reserves, the first Jewish officer in the Russian army. He might have become a lawyer, for he had begun to study law, or he could have married the daughter of a wealthy Jewish businessman who offered him a position. However, there were still restrictions upon the Jews in Russia; his heart was set on going to Palestine where he could put into practice a system of social justice.

Accompanied by a few friends, he left for Palestine in 1912. They went to Degania, the first kibbutz in Palestine, founded by Russian immigrants in the Jordan Valley, on the Sea of Galilee.

Agricultural labor was the great ideal of Degania. For this reason, Aaron David Gordon, an early hero of Israel, came there when he was almost 50, to realize his teaching of "Religion in Work." Gordon deeply affected the spiritual side of early Zionism in Palestine.

Trumpeldor did all necessary work in the kibbutz allowing no one to help him. The others soon learned not even to offer to tie his shoelaces.

Like Ben-Gurion and Ben-Zvi, Trumpeldor was driven out of Palestine by the Turks during World War I. In Alexandria, he met Vladimir Ze'ev Jabotinsky, then a correspondent for a Moscow newspaper. Both men wanted to form a Jewish army to fight on the side of the Allies. However, the British command did not want an independent Jewish army, especially one that would fight in Palestine.

General John G. Maxwell, the British commander, proposed that the Jews should organize a Corps to drive mules carrying supplies and ammunition. This Corps would be under British command, would not be a fighting unit, and would not serve in Palestine. Jabotinsky rejected these conditions. Later, in London, with Weizmann's help, he succeeded in having a Jewish Legion formed. He became a lieutenant, and his battalion fought in Palestine.

However, Trumpeldor accepted the idea of a Mule Corps, feeling that the important thing was to beat the Turks, no matter where. "All roads lead to Zion," was his thought. He enlisted and was given the title of Captain.

The Mule Corps took part in the Gallipoli campaign from May through July, 1915. Its commander was Lieutenant John Henry Patterson, who was very sympathetic toward the Jews ever since as a boy, he had devoured stories of their military leaders like Gideon, Joshua, and Judas Maccabeus. Patterson later commanded the Jewish Legion. He praised the Mule Corps highly, but in spite of its good work and courage under fire, it was disbanded in December, 1915.

However, Trumpeldor and his comrades had not worked in vain. The cause of Zionism became better known to British commanders, and the Mule Corps' activities were reported by correspondents throughout the world.

Since Trumpeldor could not serve as a regular soldier, he had the grand idea of going to Russia to enlist at least 100,000 Jewish soldiers to march overland to Transjordan. The Czar had been overthrown in the 1917 Revolution, and Trumpeldor thought he could gain the consent of the new government. When this, too, was overthrown, Trumpeldor had to give up his idea. Instead, he tried to organize groups to come to Palestine as *chalutzim*, pioneers, in collective settlements. A small number came, and he set up training centers where they could learn to work on the land.

In 1920, France, which held a mandate over Syria and Lebanon, tried to place parts of Upper Galilee under its control. Arabs loyal to the British were attacking French soldiers and Jewish colonists in the extreme north of Palestine. Moreover, Bedouins were making raids upon the settlements.

Many Jewish leaders and organizations thought that these colonies should be given up, but Trumpeldor, who had brought settlers to Galilee, declared that not a foot of soil should be given up. He himself went to Tel Hai, "Hill of Life," where he worked in the fields. He put

Lion of Judah Monument

into practice the pioneer spirit he called *Hechalutz*, the spirit of the servants of Zion, ready to do any kind of work, no matter what their previous training had been.

In his diary entry of January 9, 1920, Trumpeldor wrote that a French cavalry patrol had to retreat from Metulla, the northernmost settlement in Palestine. However, the colonists went out to work in the fields the next day, because, "It is a shame to lose time that is so valuable for sowing the wheat."

He again sent messages asking for help to save the settlements, especially Tel Hai and nearby Kfar Giladi. In a final message, he wrote that the Arabs had taken up a position on a hill only 1,000 yards from the main house at Tel Hai. They had looted Metulla the night before, but he had chased them away.

On February 29, Trumpeldor was at his defense headquarters in Kfar Giladi. While they were eating breakfast, the settlers heard shots and learned that the Arabs were attacking Tel Hai. Trumpeldor rushed there with nine men.

A small group of Arabs, led by the son of the local sheik, were demanding entrance into the house, which was surrounded by a stockade. They said they wanted to see whether any French were hiding there. The Arab leader and four followers were allowed to enter. Trumpeldor went along upstairs, but noticing that one of the Arabs had gone into the courtyard to call others in, Trumpeldor went down again.

Two girls, Deborah Dreschler and Sarah Tschisik, were upstairs guarding the supplies. Suddenly, Trumpeldor heard Deborah crying out, "They are taking my gun!" He immediately gave the order to fire. The Arabs returned the fire and threw grenades.

Rushing to the door, Trumpeldor was wounded, fought on, and was wounded twice more. Each time, he refused help and did not allow himself to be carried inside the house, but after the third wound, his friends carried him in. He spoke words of encouragement, saying that no time could be lost taking care of him. Every remark of his began with, "*Ein davar*." ("Never mind." "It is nothing." "Don't bother." "It doesn't matter.")

Although outnumbered, the defenders beat off the Arabs. The two girls and five of the men were killed. Trumpeldor was still alive, but he realized that he did not have long to live. To the doctor who had been summoned to treat his wounds, he said, "It is nothing. It is good to die for our country." As he was being carried to Kfar Giladi, he died.

Although Joseph Trumpeldor won fame as a heroic fighter, he was really a lover of peace. He hated war and wrote that war is degrading and degrades all that it touches. His greatest concerns were the attainment of social justice and the betterment of the Jewish people, but circumstances turned him into a great fighter.

The settlement of Tel Yosef (Joseph) in Galilee, a region forever associated with him in the history of Israel, was named in his honor.

On a hill near Tel Hai there is a cemetery in which those who gave up their lives at Tel Hai are buried. Here, too, are the graves of some fallen members of Hashomer and soldiers of the War of Independence. Above the graves of Trumpeldor and his companions is a statue of the Lion of Judah on which there are eight names and these words in Hebrew:

"It is good to die for our country."

This has become a place of pilgrimage for the young, who come there every year on Tel Hai Day to honor "the true and courageous fighters, men of toil and peace, who followed the plowshare and sacrificed their lives for the honor of Israel and her soil."

Those words are really the greatest memorial to Joseph Trumpeldor. His own words and heroism inspired the courageous men and women who helped build the State of Israel and set a noble example to the fighters of the War of Independence in 1948.

It is an example that is still followed. Fighting against odds, as he did, the Jewish people in Palestine, and, later, in Israel, have acted according to his slogan. To the greatest danger and suffering, even to death that may come in pursuit of noble ideals and goals, there is but one answer:

"*Ein davar.*" "Never mind. It is a small price to pay."

Joseph Trumpledor   Vladimir Ze'ev Jabotinsky

Eliezer Ben Yehuda
"Only Hebrew Spoken Here."

"Everyone—young and old—spoke Yiddish, Ladino, Russian, or Rumanian — anything but Hebrew."

So wrote David Yudelowitz, one of the Bilu, about his difficulties as he tried to teach in Hebrew at a school in Rishon Le Zion in 1885.

Yiddish, which comes from German dialects with some Hebrew and Slavic words thrown in, is the language of the Ashkenazim, descendants of the Jews who emigrated long ago to Germany and countries east of it.

Ladino, which comes from medieval Spanish, is the language of the Sephardic Jews, who lived in Spain and Portugal centuries ago.

Today, all the languages mentioned by Yudelowitz and many other languages can be heard in Israel, but for the majority of the 2,500,000 Jews there, Hebrew is the everyday language of speech, writing, books, the press, and the schools. It is also widely used in the theater, law courts, business, and public affairs. This acceptance of Hebrew has been called one of the miracles that helped create the State of Israel!

How did it come about that Hebrew, considered a dead language for almost 2,000 years, once more became a living language?

Most of the credit for bringing it to life again belongs to the almost fanatical will of one man, Eliezer Ben Yehuda, "Son of Judah." In his youth he had a vision, about which he later wrote: "A powerful inner voice called out to me: Israel must be reborn in the land of its ancestors." To him, an inseparable part of that rebirth was the coming back to life of the Hebrew language. To that he dedicated his life — neither hardships, illness, nor persecution could stop him.

Eliezer Ben Yehuda, originally Perlman, was born in Lithuania, Russia, in 1859. He attended a rabbinical school until he was 14, while he lived with an uncle in a nearby town because his parents were poor. According to a story, he was chased out of the house because his uncle found him reading a non-sacred book, a Hebrew translation of *Robinson Crusoe* someone had given him.

Afraid to go back home, Eliezer trudged along a road. A kind man, Shlomo Yonas, saw him the next day in the synagogue where the boy had spent the night. Shlomo heard his story and welcomed him to his own home as a member of his family.

Eliezer spent two happy years in the Yonas household. Shlomo's eldest daughter, Deborah, taught him French, German, and Russian. Yonas, who had a deep love of Hebrew, made the boy promise that he would always keep Hebrew alive in his mind and heart as a language of great beauty.

Eliezer left the Yonas home to go to high school in a larger town. Yonas himself suggested that he do this. The entire family was unhappy, especially Deborah, who had fallen in love with Eliezer. He promised that he would always remember her.

In high school he began to think about the freedom of the Jews from oppression and the restoration of their land, which he preferred to call Israel rather than Palestine. He thought that he had found his life's work, but he also had to think about earning a living. He decided to go to Paris to study medicine.

There he began to work for Zionism long before Herzl. He wrote an article for *Hashahar*, in which he argued that a Jewish nation must be established in *Eretz Israel*, "The Land of Israel," and that one language, Hebrew, would unite the Jews. He signed the article *Ben Yehuda*; it was the first time that he used this name.

In Paris, he learned that he had tuberculosis. A warmer place, like Algeria, was suggested, but he had no money. A friend obtained the necessary funds through an appeal to Baron Rothschild. Ben Yehuda's health improved in Algeria, and he returned to Paris.

In both places he thought more and more about the vision of the rebirth of Israel and the restoration of Hebrew. He gave up the idea of becoming a doctor so that he could work on the Hebrew language and go to live in Palestine. He felt the need of doing as much as he could rapidly since he might not live long because of his sickness.

He had been corresponding with Deborah Yonas. When he wrote her about his plans, she reminded him of his promise. He replied that he did not want to ask her to marry him because he was poor and ill, and life for her, the daughter of a well-to-do man, would be very hard in Palestine. However, she was willing to share all hardships with him, and they were married.

They went to Palestine in 1881; he began to teach her Hebrew on the way from Europe. They settled in Jerusalem. Eliezer taught Hebrew, started a Jewish weekly paper called *Hatzevi*, "The Deer," wrote Hebrew schoolbooks, and did translations into Hebrew. He formed a society called the Defenders of the Language, whose members promised to speak only Hebrew among themselves and to teach their families Hebrew.

Ben Yehuda's ideas were known in Palestine even before he came there. His article in *Hashahar* had been reprinted in many papers, and from Paris he had sent other articles to a Hebrew paper in Jerusalem. Now, his activities aroused unfriendliness and bitter opposition among orthodox religious groups who thought that Hebrew, as the language of the Old Testament and prayers, was too sacred for everyday use.

However, in other lands there were many Zionists, like Ahad Ha'am, Peretz Smolenskin, Menahem Mendel Ussishkin, and Chaim Nachman Bialik (1873-1934), who were writing in Hebrew and urging that someday Hebrew should be the popular language of the Jews in Palestine.

Bialik later addressed a Zionist Congress in Hebrew. He did not come to Palestine until 1924, but his works in Hebrew were already known to Jews all over the world. He is considered the greatest Hebrew poet after the time of Judah Halevi (1085-1140), the rabbi, philosopher, physician, and writer, who is called one of the great men of the Middle Ages. Bialik was given the titles "The Poet of His People," and "The Poet of the Hebrew Renaissance." His greatest poem is "In the City of Slaughter," written after the Kishinev pogrom of 1903; it inspired many to seek ways of self-defense or to go to Palestine.

In Palestine some of the Biluim visited Ben Yehuda and were taught by him. A number of schools began to give lessons in Hebrew.

In the meantime, Ben Yehuda kept on doing research for his dictionary. Hebrew had, of course, been a spoken language at one time; the Bible and other writings did not contain all the words the Jewish people spoke about 2,000 years ago. Ben Yehuda searched for clues that would reveal the lost words, or he formed new words that were "pure," made up only from other Hebrew words or parts of words, and that had a beautiful sound.

He printed one or two words in each issue of *The Deer*. This feature aroused great interest. Readers sent letters in which they asked for Hebrew words for new ideas and things. Ben Yehuda filled the house with scraps of paper on which he wrote his notes; he did not learn to use index cards until years later.

The strict rule of the Ben Yehuda household was, "Only Hebrew spoken here." When Deborah gave birth to their first child, Ben Yehuda made her promise that she would speak only Hebrew to him and keep him away from all who did not speak it. He called Deborah the first Hebrew mother in nearly 2,000 years and their son, Ben Zion, "Son of Zion," the first child in all that time to hear only Hebrew as an infant.

In 1887, Ben Yehuda was ill, the paper was not doing well, and he needed money for work on his dictionary. At Deborah's suggestion he went to see her family in Russia to raise money. At the Yonas home, many, including Ussishkin, came to hear him speak about his campaign for Hebrew and about life in Palestine. He received help and also promises that several young persons would go to Palestine.

Pola Yonas, Deborah's youngest sister, then about 14 years old, was very happy to see him again. She was very fond of him when he lived with her family. He was pale and thin after his illness, but Pola thought he looked romantic because of his beard and his Oriental clothes.

Soon after he returned home, he wrote articles that aroused the anger of many Palestinian Jews, especially those who lived on money sent from abroad. They got the religious authorities to place a ban on his house and *The Deer*, but he fought back. Meanwhile, Deborah, who had prepared herself while he was away, got a position teaching Hebrew in a girls' school. The head of a French society promised to get financial help from French Jews and also a regular contribution from Baron de Rothschild so that Ben Yehuda could go ahead with the work on the dictionary.

Then misfortune hit Eliezer and Deborah just as things began to go well. She became a sufferer from tuberculosis and died after a long illness at age 37, leaving five children, three of whom died a few months later. When Deborah was ill, Ben Yehuda got his mother into the country to look after her and the children. The rule about Hebrew had to be broken, and his enemies rejoiced, saying that Ben Yehuda was being punished.

In a letter to Ben Yehuda, Pola wrote that she wanted to change her first name to a Hebrew name and asked for suggestions. He sent her a list, from which she chose *Hemda*, "Cherished." Then he suggested that she change her last name by coming to the Land of Israel and becoming Mrs. Ben Yehuda. Upon the advice of his doctor and close friends he later wrote her that he still had tuberculosis and had been warned that he might not live long. Like her sister, Hemda replied that she would share his life.

Accompanied by her parents, Hemda left for Constantinople, met Ben Yehuda and married him there. He began to teach her on the voyage to Palestine.

In Jerusalem, Hemda helped Ben Yehuda get out *The Deer*. Its circulation was growing because many readers did not obey the religious ban on it but supported Ben Yehuda's views. Writers from abroad were anxious to have their articles printed in it. A Russian publisher paid Ben Yehuda for a small Hebrew dictionary.

Once again, when things were going very well, Ben Yehuda was struck a blow, this time by his enemies. They brought to the attention of the Turkish authorities an article about the Maccabees in a Hanukah issue of *The Deer*. They falsely charged that the language in it could be taken to mean that Ben Yehuda was calling for a revolt.

The article was not written by Ben Yehuda, but by Shlomo

Eliezer Ben Yehuda

Yonas, who was living in the Ben Yehuda house and was writing for the paper. However, as editor, Ben Yehuda took the responsibility. He was arrested, tried for treason, and sentenced to a year's imprisonment as a trouble-maker, but was allowed to appeal.

His friends wrote to Baron de Rothschild, who sent money to his agents in Palestine to work for Ben Yehuda's acquittal. The higher court in Beirut voted unanimously to set him free.

During this time Hemda edited *The Deer*. She offered to continue her work as editor because Ben Yehuda needed the time for the dictionary. Over his desk was a slogan: THE DAY IS SO SHORT, THE WORK TO BE DONE SO GREAT. All she wanted him to do on the paper was the feature on words and the political articles.

Ben Yehuda was elected a member of the World Zionist Organization Executive in 1897. He did not attend the First Congress because the Turkish authorities might bring harm to him and his family if he went to it. That year his work was recognized in another way. The Jewish Colonization Association gave him a large grant of money.

He paid off debts, bought new type for the paper, and also bought a larger house in which he, Hemda, her parents, who were still with them, and other relations and visitors could stay. In addition, he rented a place next door for the printing shop.

Hemda needed a rest and a change of scene. She had suffered from malaria and rheumatism. At the advice of their doctor, Ben Yehuda took her on a trip to Europe. He did research in the great libraries of London and Paris. He and Hemda met important men like Max Nordau and Israel Zangwill. Ben Yehuda saw Baron Rothschild, whom he thanked for his help, and Narcisse Leven, founder of the *Alliance Israélite Universelle*, who promised financial help for the work on the dictionary.

On their way home, they stopped in Constantinople. There Ben Yehuda met with Turkish authorities. The permit to publish *The Deer* had to be renewed, but the officials did not want to give it to Ben Yehuda because of his arrest for "inciting to a revolt." It was suggested that Hemda go back to Jerusalem, apply for a permit in her own name and send it to Constantinople.

So, Ben Yehuda was left alone. He had to give bribes, called *baksheesh*, just to see officials to find out what was going on. He also was active as a Zionist, since this was the time that Herzl was trying to purchase Palestine from the Sultan.

Ben Yehuda stayed on in Constantinople for eight months. Most of the time he was ill, weakened by tuberculosis and the strain of work. However, when he felt well enough to travel again, he went to Vienna.

He felt that he must see Herzl, whom he had missed on his journey through Europe.

The two men met and talked about Zionism. They did not agree on the program for the Jews in Palestine. Herzl thought that the matter of Hebrew as the common language could be settled after the Jews had been in Palestine for a few generations. Ben Yehuda then went to Paris to see Dr. Nordau again.

When Ben Yehuda returned home, he was discouraged about the prospects of a Jewish national home, but he was cheered by good news also. Hemda had been given permission to publish a paper in her own name. She gave it a harmless title, *The Review (Hashkafah* in Hebrew), in order not to arouse the Turkish officials. However, the contents were the same as those of *The Deer*.

Hemda was a heroic woman of remarkable ability and devotion. She was only 20 when she married Ben Yehuda, who was then 34, and she became the mother of six children, two of whom died when young. She became his most ardent helper in all his writing and political activities, went about Palestine and Europe to raise money for the dictionary, endured hardships and suffering for his sake. She lived until 1951, dying at the age of 82.

In 1901, although Ben Yehuda was weak and frail, conditions were otherwise favorable for him to devote all his time to the dictionary. His enemies were quiet, he had gained many supporters, and was receiving financial support, like the monthly sum from Baron de Rothschild.

Ben Yehuda was more than 40 years old, the work ahead of him might take 20 years, and he decided to devote all his time and energy to the task. The motto above his desk reminded him constantly of the greatness of the work to be done and the shortness of the time. Moreover, readers of the paper were asking when would the dictionary come out. Finally, he set himself to working at least 17 hours a day!

Some dictionaries are the work of one man, like the Englishman, Dr. Samuel Johnson, the American, Noah Webster, and the Frenchman, Pierre Larousse. Ben Yehuda's task was even harder than those they had faced. They worked with a spoken, living language; he worked with a "book" language that had stopped growing many centuries ago. For example, Ben Yehuda pointed out to Hemda that Hebrew did not even have a word for *dictionary!*

He had to build up a language by creating new words or finding words that had long dropped out of use. If he could not get words from parts of Hebrew words, he was willing to draw on languages related to Hebrew, like Arabic. He learned Arabic, Aramaic (a Semitic language once

Ben Yehuda

Bezalel Museum

Bialik

spoken by the Hebrews), Assyrian, Coptic (a dead language coming from ancient Egyptian), ancient Egyptian itself, and Ethiopian. For research purposes, his knowledge of English, French, German, and Russian was useful.

When Herzl died in 1904, Ben Yehuda was so depressed that he was ready to give up all work. However, Hemda encouraged him to carry on and borrowed money for a trip to Berlin where she found a publisher for the first volume, which was dedicated to the Great Benefactor, Baron Edmond de Rothschild.

Soon after Hemda returned from Berlin, there was a triple celebration in the Ben Yehuda home: the 25th anniversary of his coming to Jerusalem, his 50th birthday, and the acceptance of the first volume for printing.

That volume is a monumental work. Each word is translated into English, French, and German. There is a complete history of every word, together with quotations showing where it can be found in literature, synonyms, related words, and references to other languages, including Greek and Latin.

Ben Yehuda could now apply himself to the other volumes. His campaign was making great headway. Opposition to his program of "Hebrew instruction in Hebrew" was coming not from religious groups as much as from those who wanted French and German used. However, in the course of time, Hebrew won out.

When the great wave of immigration, the Second Aliyah, came in 1906, many in it, like Ben-Gurion and Ben-Zvi, worked for the acceptance of Hebrew.

Later, Ben Yehuda found another supporter in Vladimir Ze'ev Jabotinsky, well known as a military and political figure. He was also a student of languages who visited Ben Yehuda. When Jabotinsky was imprisoned by the British in 1920, he spent part of his time translating a few Sherlock Holmes stories into Hebrew. Later, he and a few friends started a firm with plans to publish Hebrew books for children; among the works they had in mind were translations of the Sherlock Holmes stories, *Gulliver's Travels, Robinson Crusoe,* and *Uncle Tom's Cabin.*

Among other friends who helped Ben Yehuda was the artist Boris Schatz (1866-1932), who had come from Russia and opened the first art school and museum in Jerusalem in 1906. Schatz called this Bezalel after the Biblical divinely inspired craftsman, art teacher, and builder of the Tabernacle in the wilderness. Schatz himself inspired the early generation of craftsmen and painters of Israel. The old Bezalel Museum has been replaced by a beautiful new building which is a national museum, a part of the Israel Museum.

Ben Yehuda, Hemda, and their three youngest children spent the years of World War I (1914-1918) in the United States. He could not work at ease in Jerusalem, and his political views in favor of Zionism could not be expressed in *The Review* without bringing on swift punishment by the Turks. After many difficulties, Ben Yehuda, Hemda, and the three girls arrived in New York. He had to leave his notes behind in a safe place in Jerusalem.

In New York, he did research in libraries and met Zionist leaders and groups to whom he spoke about the dictionary and the need of supporting the Allies. He was given financial aid, including a grant of $10,000 with which to build a house where he could work in peace.

When he returned to Jerusalem in 1919, he was an honored member of the *Yishuv*, the Jewish community, for his work in Hebrew and for his activities as a devoted Zionist. He had written stirring appeals to the Jewish people that won the admiration of Chaim Weizmann. His campaign for Hebrew had made great strides. Teachers of Hebrew were in great demand. Under the British Mandate, Hebrew, along with Arabic and English, was declared an official language of Palestine.

Volume Five of the dictionary was complete. Ben Yehuda had replaced the slogan: THE DAY IS SO SHORT; THE WORK TO BE DONE SO GREAT, with MY DAY IS LONG; MY WORK IS BLESSED. He was free at last to devote himself entirely to the completion of his great work, but in 1922, he died suddenly; the disease from which he had suffered so long finally conquered him. His death was mourned for three days in Palestine.

Ben Yehuda left enough notes with which others could complete the dictionary. Eight more volumes were put out with the help of Hemda, their children, and a few organizations, like the Ben Yehuda Memorial Trust; the final three of the 16 were published with the help of the Israeli Government. Of course, work on the modern Hebrew language did not stop with the death of Ben Yehuda. For example, new words have had to be formed for inventions and scientific discoveries made since his time. The growth and use of Hebrew go on; Ben Yehuda gave direction and showed the way.

The last word that he himself worked on in full was *nefesh*, Hebrew for *soul*. His was the soul of a man who was devoted to an ideal — that the Hebrew language was the means of unifying the Jewish people as a nation — and who strove heroically until he achieved that ideal. His work and its results are his monument and his memorial.

Hannah Senesh
"Blessed Is the Match."

In the struggle for human dignity and freedom, many heroes and heroines have given up life itself. A young poetess who took part in the fight against the Nazis in World War II wrote a Hebrew poem in which she compared the life of a human being who makes such a sacrifice to a match that is consumed, or burnt up, as it lights a flame. The flame that is ignited by that human being is the fire of liberty.

The name of this poetess is Hannah Senesh, who was born in Budapest, Hungary, on July 7, 1921. Her father died when she was very young. There were two children, Hannah and her brother. She went to a Hebrew and a Hungarian school and did well in both. Hannah began to write poems and keep a diary, in which the first entry is dated September 7, 1934.

Hitler's coming into power strengthened her belief in Zionism, and when she was 18, she went to Palestine. There she was sent to the agricultural school at Nahalal. The classes went on hikes in other parts of Palestine. On one of these hikes, she was stirred by a visit to Kfar Giladi and other places in Galilee associated with Joseph Trumpeldor. They awoke in her a feeling that she had a mission, but she did not yet know what it was.

After she completed the two-year course at Nahalal, she went to the kibbutz of Sdot Yam near Caesarea. There she worked in the laundry, took care of poultry, and mended fishing nets. She continued to write her diary as well as a play and poems in Hebrew. Then the idea came to her that she must go back to Hungary, organize a Youth Aliyah to get the young people into Palestine, and get her mother out of Hungary. That was to be her mission!

Soon she received a chance to go to Hungary. The British were organizing parachute units of Jews who could speak the languages of the countries of Central Europe occupied by the Nazis. Many Allied flyers who had been shot down were either in hiding or had been taken prisoner. The British wanted the Jewish volunteers to gather information and help the airmen escape to safety. The Jews also wanted to help other Jews flee from Hitler's persecution.

Hannah volunteered and was accepted. Years before, another girl, Sarah Aaronsohn, sister of Aaron, had worked in the secret group that he had formed at Zichron Ya'akov to aid British Intelligence against the Turks and Germans in World War I. Hannah's work would be even more dangerous.

The final entry in her diary is dated January 11, 1944, and says in part, "This week I go to Egypt....I am a soldier. I want to believe that what I am doing and shall do is right. The rest, time will tell."

She gave her writings, including the diary, to the kibbutz and left for training in Egypt. On March 11, 1944, she was sent to Italy, and a few days later, she (the only girl in the group) and five men, all wearing British uniforms, were flown to Jugoslavia. They parachuted to a spot near a group of partisans, underground fighters against Hitler. One of the group, Reuben Daphne, was to work with the partisans to rescue downed airmen; she and others were to get into Hungary.

Meanwhile, the Germans occupied the section of Hungary where Hannah was supposed to enter. Her group now had to walk about 200 miles at night to a different place held by partisans who would try to get her into Hungary. Another group of parachutists arrived, among whom was Joel Nussbacker. His mission was to organize underground resistance by the Jews, but he was taken prisoner when he reached Budapest.

Hannah crossed into Hungary on June 9, 1944. When her escorts were trying to find guides for her, they were arrested, and one of them committed suicide. The people of the village where Hannah was hiding became frightened and told the police about her. She was arrested, her radio set which she had hidden in a field was found by the police, and Hannah was taken to Budapest for questioning.

In spite of torture, she would not reveal any information. She showed the same courage and determination as Sarah Aaronsohn in 1917, who did not yield to the horrible torture inflicted upon her by the Turks. Sarah had shot herself rather than have any information forced out of her; Hannah resolved to face her torturers to the end.

The police found out where Hannah's mother was living and brought her to the prison. Mrs. Catherine (Katrina) Senesh had no idea that Hannah was in Budapest. She thought that Hannah and her brother, who had gone to Palestine a few years after Hannah did, were safe in Palestine. When the police questioned her about Hannah, she told them that her daughter was in Haifa. A police official then told Mrs. Senesh that Hannah was in the next room and that if the mother did not get her to talk, they might never see each other again.

It was a horrifying meeting. Hannah had been beaten, her face was bruised, and a tooth had been knocked out. Yet, she kept calm and revealed nothing. Mrs. Senesh was released, but a few days later, the Gestapo, the brutal Nazi police, arrested her and questioned her for several days.

They were finally convinced that she did not know anything about Hannah's activities, but they sent her to a prison and later sent Hannah to the same prison. Mother and daughter used to meet occasionally for a few

Hannah Senesh

moments. Four months later, Mrs. Senesh was set free. After the war, she went to live in the same kibbutz where Hannah had lived.

Hannah was questioned many times, but each time she bravely gave no information about her mission or her companions. She was put on trial before a civil court. She answered the judges courageously and refused to ask for mercy. They sent her back to jail without passing sentence at once, but early in November she was notified that she had been sentenced to die.

On the morning of November 7, Mrs. Senesh left her home early to visit her daughter. As she waited in the room of the officer in charge, she heard a shot. The firing squad had put an end to the life of Hannah Senesh, who died bravely, refusing to have her eyes bandaged, and facing her executioners erect and unflinching.

We learn about the last days of Hannah Senesh from the account given by her mother and the story by Joel Nussbacker, who made a daring escape from a moving train as he was being taken to a concentration camp.

Hannah's best-known poem was written about six months before her death; there is a story that she handed it to Reuben Daphne as they parted to go on their separate missions. This poem, especially the first line, inspired the Jews of Palestine of her generation.

Blessed is the match that is consumed in kindling the flame.
Blessed is the flame that burns in the most secret depths of the heart.
Blessed is the heart with strength to stop its beating for honor's sake.
Blessed is the match that is consumed in kindling the flame.

The Hannah Senesh House was built as a memorial to her at Sdot Yam, where she lived in Palestine.

Great honor was paid to her memory when her body was moved from a cemetery in Budapest and placed in the Israeli Military Cemetery in Jerusalem. In one section there are the graves of those who died in and near Jerusalem during the War of Independence. Another section is reserved for the parachutists, who, like Hannah Senesh, died in Europe. Not far away is the grave of Theodor Herzl on Mt. Herzl.

In another poem Hannah Senesh had written that she loved song and light and did not want the destruction and darkness of war in which she was fated to live. She expressed the wish that she might live in her own land, but that if she had to die, she might die there.

She died in the land in which she had been born, and lived for only a short time in the land she had learned to call her own. She came home to rest among the heroes and heroines of Israel, and lives in the memory of her people there.

Hannah Senesh House, Sdot Yam

Mickey Marcus
"A Soldier for All Humanity"

One day in December, 1947, a visitor entered the law office of David Daniel Marcus, nicknamed Mickey, on Fifth Avenue, New York City. He introduced himself as Major Shlomo Shamir of Haganah. He was seeking someone with the ability to get along with people and with military experience to examine the needs of the Jewish fighting forces and make recommendations for their organization.

Shamir had a list of possible choices. Mickey Marcus had been suggested to him by American Zionists who thought that Mickey could help Shamir get in touch with the right man. Mickey tried hard but could not find anybody who was available or whom Shamir and he himself thought capable.

Marcus was born on February 22, 1901. After attending Boys High in Brooklyn, where he was voted the best athlete, excelling in track, basketball, baseball, and football, he entered West Point. There he won the intercollegiate welterweight (135-147 pounds) boxing championship and his letter as a gymnast.

He was not tall but was stockily built, with heavy shoulders, a large chest, and powerful arms. He was dark-skinned, with black hair, dark eyes, and he had a most cheerful nature.

Scholastically, Mickey Marcus was in the top third in his class, the class of 1924, which was the largest up to his time and known as the Thundering Herd because of its size. He received special citations in military strategy, the study of campaigns, and leadership potential.

After serving as second lieutenant and studying law, he resigned from the army, married Emma Chaison, a teacher in the New York City public schools, and worked as a law clerk. After passing the bar examinations, Mickey took a position in the United States District Attorney's office in New York. His work was so successful that Mayor Fiorello La Guardia offered him the post of Deputy Commissioner of Correction to fight against crime and corruption. In April, 1940, Marcus became the Commissioner in charge of the prison systems of New York City.

When Hitler's power grew, Marcus gave up a promising political and law career and went back to the army as a lieutenant colonel. He felt that the United States would soon be at war with Germany and that

Hitler's attack upon the Jews was a war against all humanity.

Although he would much rather have taken part in the fighting, he was advised, because of his legal experience, to join the Judge Advocate's Department. However, he received permission to train troops in maneuvers, and after Pearl Harbor, he joined his division in Hawaii, where he organized and trained a Rangers School.

In the spring of 1943, the Pentagon transferred him to Washington where he worked under Major General John H. Hilldring, to whom he became indispensable. Mickey worked at top speed, analyzed in a few hours problems that others took days to study, could work for 16 hours at a stretch, or do with only four hours of sleep. He was promoted to the rank of colonel.

Marcus was an adviser at most of the important conferences held with the heads of Allied countries, as at Yalta, drew up the surrender plans for Italy and Germany, and selected lawyers, judges, and prosecutors for the trials of war criminals at Nuremberg.

He also managed to get into the fighting in a way that shows his determination and courage. He was sent to England to straighten out some difficulties in the Civil Affairs Division of the Supreme Headquarters Allied Expeditionary Forces. While there, he got on a transport plane, and, although he had never parachuted before, on D-Day, June 6, 1944, landed in Normandy, where he took part in the fighting. Back in Washington, General Hilldring missed him so much that he had him tracked down and brought back!

Colonel Marcus received many decorations for his services, including the Distinguished Service Medal and the award as Honorary Commander of the British Empire. After the end of the war, he could have remained in service as Brigadier General, but he felt he owed it to his wife to return to civilian life. He bought a home in Flatbush, Brooklyn, took office space in Manhattan, and was settling down to building up a law practice when Major Shamir's visit changed the course of his life—at almost 47.

Marcus's name was on Shamir's list, but Shamir had not asked him to go to Palestine. Mickey was not a Zionist, and Shamir wanted to know more about him. As he and other representatives of the Palestinian Jews spoke to him many times and began to know him well, they realized that Mickey was the man they needed, and they asked him to go to Palestine.

In turn, Mickey felt that he had to go. His mind went back to the corpses he had seen at Dachau after the Allies marched into Germany. He

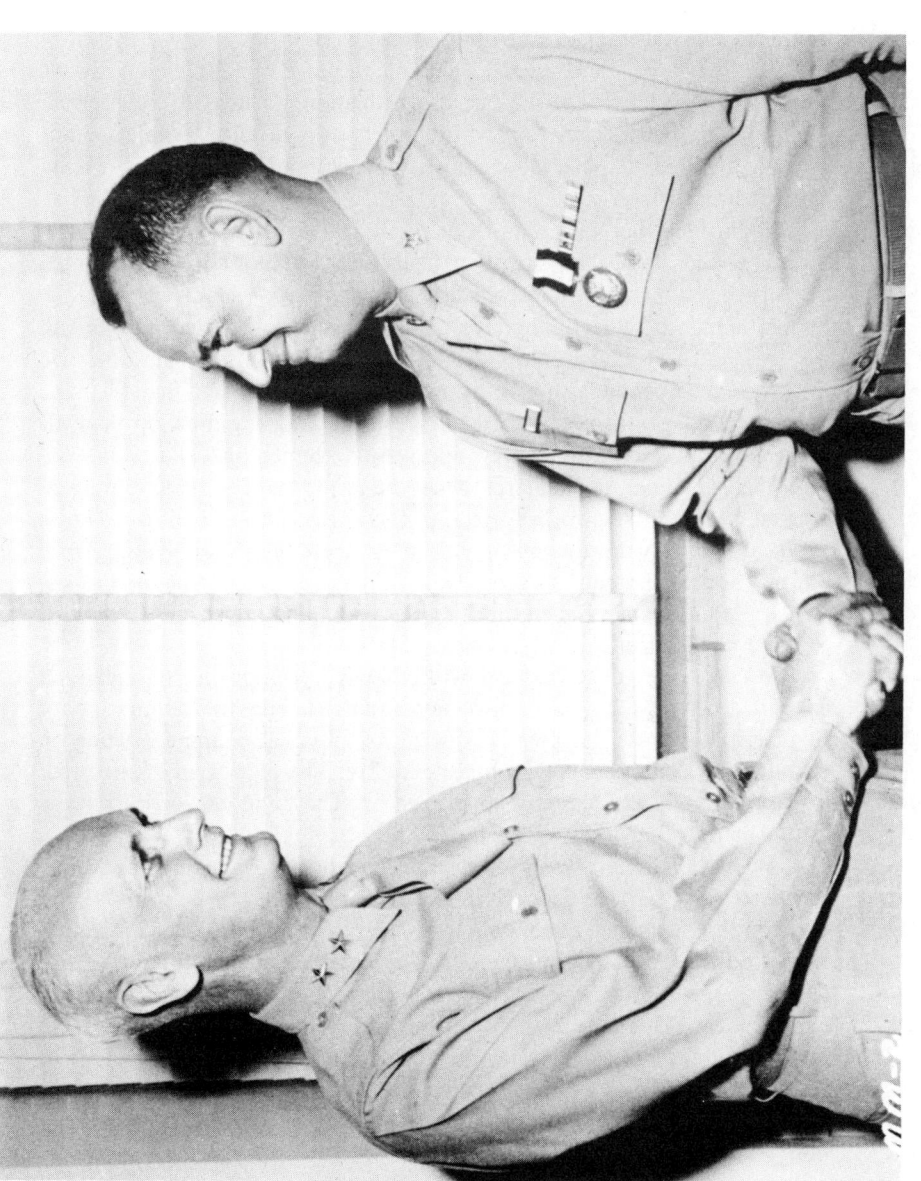

Mickey Marcus receiving Distinguished Service Medal from General Hilldring

thought of the ragged and starved survivors of the horrible concentration camps, refugees with but one dream and hope—to have a land of their own where they would no longer be wanderers, where they could live free from persecution.

First, he talked it over with his wife, who agreed because she knew that he would be unhappy if he did not go and that he would always feel that he had failed to accomplish a mission—to help the oppressed. Then he cleared the matter with government officials, who did not object, provided that he acted unofficially without publicizing his army and government services.

From his talks with Major Shamir, Mickey realized that the Jewish forces lacked up-to-date army manuals. He would have taken United States army manuals with him, since they were not secret. However, the British Mandate was still in effect, and Marcus knew that the British customs officials might not let these manuals into Palestine. He therefore memorized as much as he could and arranged that Shamir's agents should get copies in. Later, in Palestine, Mickey drew up manuals that were translated into Hebrew and were extremely useful.

Near the end of January, 1948, he came to Tel Aviv, posing as Mickey Stone, a steelworker. He met David Ben-Gurion and got to know about or work with the military leaders, men like Yigal Allon, Israel Carmi, Moshe Dayan, Yaakov Dori, Chaim Herzog, Chaim Laskov, Itzhak Rabin, Itzhak Sadeh, and Yigael Yadin. Major Shamir came back to serve at the front.

Mickey offered his services without pay, acting as an observer and adviser. The way he sized up every situation won the admiration of Ben-Gurion. Mickey advised a system of physical training, setting an example by his boxing and gymnastic ability. The men soon learned that he did not talk like a textbook instructor. They and the officers loved "the American," as they called him.

He stressed the value of discipline and organization, and above all, the need of a staff of properly trained commanders. He said that under the conditions facing them, the Jewish army must be like a razor that strikes quickly, cleanly, and sharply. The Jewish army had the blade, the fighters, but it still needed a handle—well-trained, top-flight commanders. There were able leaders, but they were not yet ready to act on Marcus's idea because they could not withdraw good men for training as commanders.

Mickey's restless spirit craved action, but Ben-Gurion did not want him to risk his life. However, he did manage to visit the scenes of

Mickey Marcus

fighting. He was making a great contribution to the Palestinian army when a message came from his wife, who had become ill, calling upon him to return home.

Noticing how gloomy the men looked when he was about to leave, Mickey cheerfully promised, "When the Arabs strike, I'll be here again." He arrived in New York in April, 1948, and his return helped his wife, Emma, to regain her health. However, he could not get the thought of the brave men he had left behind out of his mind. Then a cable came from Palestine, but he did not want to leave Emma against her wishes.

Moshe Sharett of the Jewish Agency and Mrs. Sharett met Mickey and Emma. Sharett put the case before her, explaining how much Mickey was needed, how only he had the leadership to help the Jews in Palestine in their desperate situation, and how all looked upon him as a teacher, guide, and friend. On May 2, 1948, Mickey flew to Tel Aviv.

He plunged into action at once. He inspected the battle fronts advised holding on to the Negev, and even took part in the action there when Egyptian planes attacked. Marcus stressed the value of "Attack! Attack!" Itzhak Rabin declared that under the guidance of Marcus, the Palmach had its first experience with real offensive tactics that later broke the back of the Arab Legion.

A military writer in Jerusalem wrote that Marcus changed the Israeli forces from guerrilla bands to a regular army. Later, Abba Eban said that because of the work of Marcus, when the Arabs attacked in force, "Israel was now ready on every front."

Mickey Marcus was in Tel Aviv when the state of Israel was declared. He wrote a letter to Emma to tell her that his eyes were full when he heard Ben-Gurion read Israel's Declaration of Independence.

Both Yadin and Marcus thought that other areas were of greater strategic importance than Jerusalem, but Ben-Gurion wanted the city held at all costs for the sake of morale. He declared that the Jewish people could not suffer a third destruction—after the fall of the First and Second Temples.

Mickey was sent to Jerusalem on May 25 to organize its defense. The situation was critical. The Arab Legion, led by an Englishman, John Glubb, known as Glubb Pasha, had already taken possession of the Old City. In Jerusalem, Mickey learned the motto of the troops, their answer to the question why they fought against what looked like the impossible instead of retreating. Their answer, in the spirit of the Maccabees, was always, *"Ein breira [ayn breira],"* "No choice," "No alternative."

Mickey understood and admired such spirit. Like Don Quixote, to whom he was often compared, he reached for the impossible dream, but unlike him, he knew how to face reality. What is more, in Israel, he had seen how such dreams can be made to come true!

The leaders of the different fighting groups did not always agree. Ben-Gurion decided that there had to be a unified command. He thought that a man without ties to any group could serve best. Only one man had all the qualifications—Mickey Marcus.

After an emergency meeting of the Cabinet of the Provisional Government, Mickey Stone, as Marcus was officially called, was granted a commission dated May 28, 1948 making him Supreme Commander of three brigades on the Jerusalem front. He was actually a Brigadier General; before this time nobody had held this rank in the Palestinian or Israeli army.

The defenders of the New City might not have been able to hold out much longer because the Arabs had cut off the main road from Tel Aviv on which supplies could be brought to them. There was another road, but it was not passable all the way. Jeeps could go over part of this road consisting of dirt trails and dry river beds, if pushed over some very rough spots. A very small amount of supplies could then be transferred to these jeeps from vehicles coming part of the way from Tel Aviv.

Marcus, assisted by a scout, Amos Chorev, and a few officers, examined this road and decided that it must be widened all the way. Overcoming the objections of engineers, he enlisted the aid of Ben-Gurion and Yadin, got hundreds of workers together, and work started. This had to be done at night to escape the notice of the Arabs, and attacks were made on their positions to divert their attention. After a few days, the rocky parts were cut through, soft areas made by streams were filled in, the road was widened and completed. Supplies began to roll in!

Some persons called the new road the Burma Road, others named it the Road of Courage, and still others paid Mickey Marcus the highest tribute when they spoke of it as the Mickey Marcus Road. Whatever its name, Jerusalem was saved!

Both sides were ready to accept a month's cease-fire arranged by the United Nations to begin at 10 A.M. on June 11. The day before, Mickey went to the village of Abu Ghosh, high on a hill about eight miles west of Jerusalem, to plan the next moves with Allon. In the evening, the soldiers celebrated the coming truce with a surprise party for Mickey Marcus. Before the men turned in, orders were given for a special alert since the Arabs might attack to gain better positions before the cease-fire.

Mickey had a strange premonition that night. During the festivities he told one of his aides that he felt his luck had run out. Back in his room, he was restless and unable to fall asleep. Putting on his shorts and sandals and wrapping a sheet about him, he walked out into the cool night air. The gravel crunched beneath his feet. The sentry, a new man, on the alert, as ordered, called out in Hebrew, "Who goes there?" He later reported that he could not understand Mickey's reply and fired a warning shot into the air.

What drove Mickey on will never be known. Ever friendly, he jumped over a low stone fence, perhaps to greet the sentry, who fired again. Mickey's luck had run out; the bullet hit him in the heart. He died at 3:50 A.M., a few hours before the cease-fire, "the last victim of the bloody Jerusalem front." When the sentry learned whom he had killed, he was so upset that he had to be held back from committing suicide.

David "Mickey" Marcus, a warrior and lover of music, died on the hill where the warrior and musician whose name he bore, King David, had once danced and played on musical instruments.

Mickey's body was flown to the United States on June 30. There was a ceremony at City Hall after a cortege of 60 cars made its way from services in a Brooklyn temple. Then his body was taken to West Point, where he had once asked to be buried. Thomas E. Dewey, Governor of New York, with whom Mickey had served in the District Attorney's office, United States Government officials, Moshe Dayan and Jossi Hamburger, a famous captain of ships carrying Jewish refugees, both representing Israel, were among the important persons present.

David Ben-Gurion said about Mickey Marcus, "He was the best man we had," and sent a message to Mrs. Marcus in which he told her that her husband's military gifts and qualities of character had gained for him an undying place of honor in the history of Israel.

Mrs. Eve Kirshner, at whose home in Tel Aviv Mickey had stayed, summed up what the Israelis thought of him. In a letter to Emma Marcus, she wrote that although the soldiers were used to seeing death, nevertheless they wept when they learned that Mickey had been killed.

"He belonged," she wrote, "to those rare people whose purity brings out the best in others from the first minute.... The day of his death will remain for us a day of mourning as long as we live, and our children and grandchildren will be taught to love and admire the

American who came to our help in this desperate, difficult fight."

The cemetery of the United States Military Academy at West Point is older than Arlington National Cemetery. More than 3,000 graves mark the final resting places of fighters in all the wars in which our country has taken part.

One stone is different from the others. It bears the name of a man who fell while fighting for another country. The first and last lines of the simple inscription on this stone are:

COLONEL DAVID MARCUS
A SOLDIER FOR ALL HUMANITY

Grave of Mickey Marcus

9

Yigael Yadin
Archeologist and Warrior

In the Judean desert, rising about 1,300 feet above the southwestern shore of the Dead Sea, stands the rock-fortress of Masada, on top of which King Herod built his palace in about 35 A.D. In 73 A.D., almost 1,000 Jews, men, women, and children, known as Zealots, were occupying the palace and resisting the attempts of the Roman Tenth Legion to capture it. The Zealots, led by Eleazar Ben Ya'ir, were the last to hold out in the revolt after the destruction of the Temple by Titus in 70 A.D.

The Zealots had no thought of surrender when they realized that the Romans were finally going to break into the fortress after a long siege. In a speech full of emotion, Eleazer told his men what the Romans would do to them, their wives, and their children.

He said that it was better to die as free men than live as slaves and proposed that the men should first kill their wives and children. Then ten men picked by lot would kill all the other men. After this, the ten men would pick one man to kill the other nine. He would then set fire to everything except the food so the Romans could see that the Zealots were not overcome by lack of food, but they had chosen to die rather than surrender. Finally, the sole survivor would kill himself. This horrifying plan was carried out!

What happened inside the fortress on that tragic day has been told by the historian Josephus, who had taken part in the revolt elsewhere but had surrendered to Vespasian, whose favor he gained. It seems that there were seven survivors, two old women and five children who had hidden themselves while the self-slaughter was going on. Josephus may have received the story from these women.

Masada has become a symbol of courage to Israel and a place of pilgrimage for Israeli youth. Recruits of the armored units of the Israel Defense forces take their oath of allegiance on top of Masada and declare, "Masada shall not fall again!" A special medal struck by the Israeli Government bears those words on one side, and on the other, "We shall remain free men."

On July 7, 1969, the remains of 27 defenders who had died in the siege of Masada were dug up and buried with full military honors. One of the speakers at the ceremony said, "If we have to face our enemies again, our slogan will be not an honorable death but honor through victory, life, and freedom." However, another speaker, Professor Yigael Yadin, declared, addressing the dead heroes, "We will not judge the way you chose to preserve the honor and freedom of Israel."

It was fitting that Yigael Yadin should be a speaker at this historic

Masada Medal

site. As a warrior, he has fought for the honor and freedom of Israel, and as an archeologist, he was in charge of one of the most exciting and important excavations of modern times, which unearthed the palace of Herod at Masada and confirmed part of the story told by Josephus.

Yigael Yadin (born Sukenik) was born to become an archeologist. His father was Eleazar Sukenik, the first professor of archeology at the Hebrew University in Jerusalem. Yigael was born in 1917 in Jerusalem, a sabra, or native-born. Professor Sukenik took young Yigael with him when exploring and excavating sites. As a Boy Scout, Yigael led other Scouts on long hikes over small ancient roads, especially to hiding places mentioned in the Bible. He and the other boys learned the land thoroughly and used this knowledge later in war.

In 1930, at age 13, he joined the Haganah. While in high school, he made up his mind to become an archeologist. In 1935, he entered the Jewish University, but a year later he was called to active duty because of Arab terrorism. When the British, needing help in World War II, allowed Haganah members to become part of the unit called the Supernumerary Police, Yadin joined. He also trained Haganah men in a special school. In 1945, he left active service.

Yadin married Carmella Ruppin, who urged him to complete his studies for the Master of Arts degree, which had been interrupted by military duties. He also began to work on his doctorate, concentrating on problems of Biblical warfare.

In 1947, Ben-Gurion asked him to come back to active service because of the threat of war with the Arabs. Yadin was Chief of Staff of the Haganah in the War of Independence. He drew upon his great knowledge of archeology and the history of warfare, especially in Biblical and Roman times. Two examples stand out.

In the closing days of the war, his knowledge of ancient history helped the Israelis win an important victory by capturing a fortified position in the Negev. The fortress of Al-Auja had to be taken in order to gain possession of that important area before the cease-fire went into effect. An attack from the north seemed to be the direct way, but it would have cost many lives and taken too long. There was no apparent road from the south.

However, Yadin seemed to remember that somewhere he had read about another road. He thought and thought until he came upon the answer. Looking through his archeological notes, he found that there had been a road over which the Romans had marched — from the south! He told Allon, the commander at this front, about the possibility, and scouts were sent to see whether any traces of the old road could be found. A message came back, "Difficult, but possible."

Yigael Yadin

To escape the notice of the Egyptians, engineers worked in the darkness, placing boards and other supports for tanks and armored cars. Suddenly and unexpectedly, the Israelis burst into the fortress and compelled the Egyptians to surrender.

A similar story is told about how Yadin used his knowledge of the Bible. The United Nations had given Israel a tiny strip of land opposite Sinai along the Gulf of Aqaba, including the port of Eilat (Elath). There seemed to be no road by which the Israelis could reach Eilat. Yadin knew that in Biblical times there had been roads to it passable on foot and by camels. A survey from the air showed where a temporary road could be built. Only two days later, March 10, 1949, Eilat was in the hands of the Israelis, and Yadin sent a telegram of greetings to Ben-Gurion — from Eilat!

In the War of Independence, Israel had able military commanders on every front. Yigael Yadin, later a Major General and Chief of Staff of the Israel Defense Forces, was the link between David Ben-Gurion, Minister of Defense, and the commanders of the separate units of the armed forces.

After the end of the war, Yadin accompanied Moshe Dayan on some of the secret visits to King Abdullah of Jordan and took an active part in later negotiations with that monarch. In 1952, he retired from the army to resume his academic career and archeological research. Eventually, he became a professor of archeology at the Hebrew University in Jerusalem, like his father before him.

Yadin made some remarkable finds, of which those at Masada from 1963 to 1965 are the most noteworthy. In April, 1960, members of expeditions organized by him discovered in a cave 15 letters written by Bar Kochba, and a year later, about 40 more documents of that hero's time, about 132 A.D.

Yadin's name is linked with the Dead Sea Scrolls. (Scrolls are rolls of leather, parchment, paper, or even metal containing writing.) These scrolls contain some of the oldest written texts of parts of the Old Testament, hymns, psalms, commentaries, rules of an ancient religious sect, and the story of an imaginary war between the powers of light and darkness. Yadin's association with them came about in an unexpected manner.

As Chief of Staff of Haganah, Yadin was stationed in Tel Aviv in November, 1947, when tensions arose between the Arabs and the Jews. On a visit to Jerusalem, he went to see his parents. His father, with excitement in his voice, asked him, "What shall I do? Shall I go to Bethlehem?" Professor Sukenik explained that he had received a call a few days before from a friend in the Old City, an Armenian dealer in antiquities who said he had something interesting to show him.

They could not visit each other because Jerusalem had been divided into military zones by the British, and the professor and his friend did not have passes to move about freely. However, they did meet at the barbed wire of Military Zone B, and through the wire the dealer showed Sukenik some pieces of leather with old Hebrew writing on them and said that he had more in his shop. Sukenik managed to get a pass, entered Zone B, and saw the scraps of leather in the shop. He was interested and excited when the dealer said that another dealer in Bethlehem had the entire scrolls.

The Armenian offered to go with Sukenik to Bethlehem, but the trip could be dangerous because the Arabs held the city and the road to it. Sukenik himself was willing to take the risk, because no danger can hold back an archeologist hot on the trail of an important discovery, but his wife refused to let him go. That is how matters stood when Yigael arrived on the 28th of November.

In answer to his father's questions, Yigael, as an archeologist himself, would have answered, "Go!" As his son, he did not want him to risk his life. At the same time, Yigael felt sorry for him when he saw how disappointed he would be if he gave up the chance of acquiring such an unusual treasure in his field of study. However, as Chief of Staff of Haganah, Yadin had to advise his father not to go. He then left for Tel Aviv, but, as he himself wrote, for days he could not put the scrolls out of his mind.

Nor could his father. Without anybody's knowledge, he arranged to go to Bethlehem with the dealer. Sukenik felt that this might be his last chance, since the Arabs would become more hostile after November 29 because of the partition plan. He and his friend reached Bethlehem by bus. Sukenik was shown three scrolls, which he bought for a small sum for the Hebrew University. Carrying them in an old paper bag so as not to arouse the suspicions of petty thieves, Sukenik, together with his friend, boarded a bus filled with Arabs and reached Jerusalem in safety.

Yadin did not learn about this until about a month later. In fact, he did not know the rest of the story of Sukenik and the Dead Sea Scrolls until he read his father's private journal in 1953, soon after his father had died.

The complete story of these scrolls is a combination of mystery, secret agency, and detective tales joining together the talents of a James Bond, Secret Agent 007, and a Sherlock Holmes.

The story begins in a cave at Qumram near the Dead Sea. A Bedouin boy taking care of goats threw stones into the cave and heard an unusual sound. Returning the next day with a companion, he climbed into the cave and discovered pottery jars, which his stones had hit. In one of the jars there were rolls of leather with writing on them. The boy took the scrolls to a dealer. As word got around, other Bedouins and, later, archeologists looked in caves and found more scrolls.

In January, 1948, Sukenik was asked by an Arab friend in the Old City to look at four other scrolls. These belonged to the Syrian Monastery of St. Mark, which had bought them from a dealer, not the same one with whom Sukenik had dealt. Sukenik was allowed to take them home for examination on condition that he return them after a few days. He knew that the price of these would be very high.

After looking at them thoroughly, Sukenik realized that they belonged with the ones he had bought, and he wanted to buy them for the Hebrew University. Because of the war situation, money was not readily available. Sukenik wanted to mortgage his house, but was persuaded by friends not to do this. Negotiations for the purchase of the scrolls dragged on while he tried to reach Government officials who could help. By the time word reached Ben-Gurion, who offered to have the Government provide any sum needed, Sukenik was informed that the scrolls were no longer for sale.

The Metropolitan (like an Archbishop) of the Monastery had called in members of the American School of Oriental Research to examine the scrolls. The scholar, John C. Trever, who has told the story in *The Untold Story of Qumram*, photographed the four scrolls, and he and other scholars wrote articles about them. The Metropolitan himself then took the scrolls to the United States because they would be safer there and might bring a higher price.

In 1954, Yigael Yadin was on a lecture tour in the United States. His topic: "The Dead Sea Scrolls." On June 1, a friend, the journalist Monty Jacobs, called to tell him that there was an advertisement in *The Wall Street Journal* offering four Dead Sea Scrolls for sale. Here was a chance for Yigael to complete the collection started by his father.

The Metropolitan, a Syrian, might not be willing to have the scrolls come to Israel, especially after the War of Independence. Therefore, trusted agents carried on negotiations for Yadin without having his name appear in the deal. The four scrolls were purchased for $250,000, a sum many, many times greater than what Sukenik had paid for the first three, seven years before, or than what he might have had to pay for these in Jerusalem in 1948.

Samuel Gottesman, an American businessman, contributed $150,000; the American Fund for Israeli Institutions gave the rest. The seven Dead Sea Scrolls are now on display in a new building in

Jerusalem called the Shrine of the Book — one of the great tourist attractions of Israel.

Yigael Yadin's father had written, "Thus the Jewish people have lost a priceless heritage," when he was unable to buy the four scrolls. However, his son restored that heritage to Israel.

Yadin has written many articles on archeology in scholarly magazines. He is the author of books that show his interests: *The Message of the Scrolls; War of the Sons of Light against the Sons of Darkness* (edition and explanation of one of the three scrolls bought by his father); *The Art of Warfare in Biblical Lands; Masada, Herod's Fortress and the Zealots' Last Stand*. He has won several awards for his scholarship, such as the Israel Prize in Jewish Studies and the Rothschild Prize in Humanities.

Yigael and Carmella Yadin have two daughters. In 1967, a few members of the Government wanted him to be appointed Defense Minister, but he supported the choice of Dayan.

Although Yigael Yadin has reached the top level of military command, he is, like so many other Israeli military leaders, a man of peace. He has served his country well in academic halls and military ranks, an Israeli hero of war and archeology.

Shrine of the Book

10

Yigal Allon
Redoubtable, Bold, and Imaginative

These are some of the words that have been used to describe Yigal Allon. To them can be added "courageous, cool, and fearless." He had to show bravery ever since he was a boy. One of the stories told about him is that on his *bar mitzvah*, his 13th birthday, when a Jewish boy is considered to be a man, his father gave him a Turkish pistol as a present. The family lived in a settlement that was often raided by Arabs who came at night to steal livestock and crops. His father sent Yigal out that night to patrol the field alone.

When three Arab horsemen came to take away stacks of grain, Yigal challenged them. From behind him, a shot rang out, and a voice cried out in Arabic, "You robbers, I'll kill every one of you!" The Arabs fled. The person who had fired the shot was Yigal's father, who had hidden himself behind a tree to see how his son would behave. He assured Yigal that he had passed the test, for he had showed no fear and was now truly a man!

Yigal's grandparents had helped settle Rosh Pina, an old farming community in Upper Galilee. His parents moved to Kfar Tabor, where Yigal was born in 1918. He is a sabra with roots that go deep into the soil.

The word *sabra* has been used before in this book to refer to a native-born Israeli. It is the name of the fruit of a cactus that is soft, tender, and sweet on the inside but tough and thorny on the outside and hard for anybody to crush.

Yigal's last name was originally Peicovitch. He was the youngest of six children, five boys and a girl. All the children had to work on the farm as soon as they could because the soil was hard, rocky, and dry. Life at Kfar Tabor was that of true pioneers — one of backbreaking toil and often surrounded by danger.

Reuben Peicovitch, Yigal's father, organized self-defense units against the Bedouins and other unfriendly Arabs. His Arab neighbors learned to respect him and even became friendly to him and his family. He believed in getting along with them on peaceful terms, if possible, learning their language and understanding their ways. He passed this lesson on to Yigal and sent him to the home of an Arab friend to spend his vacation with the friend's son, a boy of Yigal's age. In return, the Arab boy often spent time with the Peicovitch family. Yigal learned to speak Arabic well, and his knowledge of Arab ways proved useful to him later on.

Yigal's mother died when he was five, and his sister left high

Dayan, Sadeh, and Allon, 1938

school to take care of the family. Yigal went to a communal school until he was 14 but worked before and after school hours. When he finished his early schooling, he had to take up the burden of farm work because his father was ill. When there was not much to do on the farm, he worked on government roads. Then, as his sister married, and all his brothers moved away, he and his father were left to run the farm by themselves.

Yigal was anxious to study scientific agriculture. Fortunately, a new school, the Kadourie School, had been set up near Kfar Tabor. Yigal passed the entrance examinations and received a two-year scholarship.

At age 16, he joined the Haganah. He had two days off a week for training. The young trainees used the Bible as a military manual, learning about the battles described in it. They could see some of the Biblical battlefields as they trained near Tabor, the mountain and valley where Gideon and Deborah had fought.

At the end of a year, Allon was chosen to attend a summer camp for the training of noncommissioned officers. At the end of that summer, he returned home as a section commander of his village. In 1938, he took a three-month officers' course. One of his fellow-students was Moshe Dayan. Six months later, Allon himself was an officer and an instructor in that camp. Yigael Yadin was one of his students.

When an elite corps, the *Palmach,* "Spearhead," was organized as the striking force of the Haganah, with Itzhak Sadeh as its commander, Allon, who was in his early 20's, was made the top executive officer. He selected strong, hardy young men from the kibbutzim, gave them rigid training under battle conditions, and led daring, unexpected attacks against Arab raiders.

The Haganah and Palmach helped the British when the Vichy French in Syria and Lebanon threatened to invade northern Palestine. Allon sent dark-skinned Sephardic Jews who could speak Arab fluently and knew the country well into Syria as scouts. They returned with the needed information.

One detachment serving with the British, consisting of Australians, with whom Allon went into Syria, did not follow his instructions but became separated from his Palmach unit. Allon bluffed the Vichy French invaders into thinking that they were surrounded by a large force. Finally, he and his men had to retreat under cover of darkness. Fortunately, Allon knew the way back very well. He took charge, managed to get the Australians together, and led them back safely, even taking a few French prisoners. The Australian commander offered Allon a reward and was shocked when he refused to take any money, saying that his men were not fighting for pay, but for their homes, and were ready to serve again when needed!

At the end of World War II in 1945, Yaakov Dori, the Haganah Chief of Staff, went to the United States to buy arms, and Sadeh took his place. Allon now became acting commander of the Palmach, at age 27. The Palmach had grown to 6,000 men. When the British limited immigration, Palmach youth were among those who went to Europe, organized the escape of refugees, manned ships to run the British blockade, and succeeded in getting many thousand refugees into Palestine. The Palmach protected landing places, freed prisoners held by the British, and fought off British troops and police.

When Dori returned from the United States in 1947, he resumed his post as Chief of Staff of Haganah. Sadeh wanted Allon to remain as commander because of his ability; he himself took another post. Yigael Yadin, a former student of Allon, became Chief of Staff of Haganah when Dori became ill.

The Arabs prepared to attack after the announcement of the partition plan, the end of the British Mandate, and the withdrawal of British troops. Allon was put in charge of the Galilee region, familiar to him. Yadin and Ben-Gurion allowed him to attack Safed, an ancient city of Galilee.

Control of this city was absolutely necessary, because, situated about 2,600 feet high, it was a supply base and dominated the highway from Haifa across Galilee. The British troops had withdrawn on April 16, 1948; about 20,000 Syrians immediately seized a large part of the city, the higher section. The lower section was occupied by a small Jewish garrison, about 35 Palmach youth, and fewer than 2,000 inhabitants, most of them old persons, women, and children. The Arabs on the heights and in the Arab quarter were able to fire down on the Jewish quarter and were starving the people there into surrender by a blockade.

Allon had a bold plan calling for skill and expert timing. He decided not to defend small Jewish settlements but to seize Arab key points, forts, and roads near Safed, and then make a direct attack on the largest stronghold, Safed itself. After Safed had been taken, the rest of Galilee could be cleared of Arabs.

First, by surprise attacks and unexpected maneuvers, Allon took some of the villages and strong points around Safed. In one village he won the support of an old Arab who had known his father and did not sympathize with the aims of the Arab "liberators" because his village had suffered at their hands in the past. He received Allon warmly, recognized who he was, and told him where the Arabs were encamped.

Yigal Allon

His father's lessons that Yigal should learn Arabic and get to understand the Arabs certainly paid off this time.

Allon was not yet ready to attack Safed, but he felt that the small garrison inside needed something to boost their morale. With a small group he made his way through the Arab lines at night, entered Safed, and by his presence, encouraged the defenders to hold out, promising deliverance in three days. He kept his promise. Safed was taken, and the Arabs fled.

When Israel was declared an independent state, Allon heard the news while he was still in the field. A full-scale war was now on. He swept the Arabs from northern Galilee and took part in the capture of the Negev in an operation called Ten Plagues, after the plagues that came upon the Egyptians when Moses led the Israelites out of Egypt.

After the end of the war, Allon left the army as a Brigadier General and went back as a farmer to the kibbutz of Genossar (Ginosar), of which he is a founder and where he has made his home since 1937. He then went to England to study economics. In 1954, he entered politics, forming a small political party, and in 1955, he was elected to the Knesset. He was Minister of Labor from 1961 to 1968.

Prime Minister Levi Eshkol, Golda Meir, and other government leaders wanted Yigal Allon to be Minister of Defense in the expected 1967 War with the Arabs. However, the public had begun to look upon him as a political figure and wanted Moshe Dayan, who had become better known as a military man because of his leadership in the 1956 war.

When Eshkol died in March, 1968, Allon became Acting Prime Minister until Golda Meir was chosen as Eshkol's successor. He then became Deputy Prime Minister and Minister of Immigrant Absorption.

Blue-eyed, sandy-haired, of medium height, Allon is a handsome looking man with strong features. He is a very forceful and convincing speaker with a charming, direct manner of presenting his views, especially on how to treat the Arabs in territory occupied by the Israelis.

A great military leader when still a young man, Allon is now called "the farmer-politician." He is still truly a son of the soil, one who has never really left the farm but has continued to work in Genossar when he is not busy with public duties. Predictions have been made that some day he will reach the top rung of his career — as Prime Minister.

11
Moshe Dayan
An Ideal Sabra and Born Leader: "Follow Me!"

In June, 1967, photographs, drawings, and cartoons of a man with a black patch over his left eye began to appear in many countries. Books and articles were written calling him one of the great military leaders of modern times. This man is Moshe Dayan, Israel's Minister of Defense during the Six-Day War against the Arabs.

Moshe Dayan has been called the ideal sabra, the native-born leader that Israel needed. He was born in Degania on May 20, 1915. His parents, Shmuel and Dvora Dayan, were among the earliest settlers in the kibbutz of Degania.

In 1921, Shmuel Dayan moved his family to the Valley of Jezreel to help found the moshav of Nahalal. A moshav is a cooperative community that differs from a kibbutz in allowing private ownership.

A village school was set up in which Moshe received an elementary education. While still in school, he got a taste of military service. At age 12, he did sentry duty against Bedouins who came to plunder. At 14, he joined the Haganah.

Dayan was used to danger from his earliest days. He recently recalled that his first childhood memory, when he was five and still at Degania, was the day the Arabs set fire to the kibbutz. "There was fighting, incidents all the time," he said. "Our situation was considerably more dangerous than it is now."

A women's organization had opened a secondary agricultural school for girls in Nahalal. Since there was no high school for boys in or near Nahalal, parents asked that their sons be admitted. Permission was granted, and Moshe was the first boy to enter.

During his student days, he continued to serve in Haganah. At 18, he himself trained Haganah recruits. Dayan did not attend college; he was too busy to devote time to study until years later.

In July, 1935, he married Ruth Schwarz, whom he had met at the school. She was the daughter of a lawyer in Jerusalem and was attending the school because she wanted to become a farmer's wife. To this day, she calls herself a farmer's wife! After a honeymoon in England, they settled down in their own hut in Nahalal. Since Moshe's parents were busy with political affairs in other parts of Palestine, he also took care of their farm. Dayan still thinks of himself as a farmer.

Itzhak Sadeh had organized Haganah units called field platoons and appointed Dayan and Allon platoon leaders. Sadeh looked upon the two of them as his favorites. Dayan also joined the Supernumerary Police Corps while continuing to work in Haganah.

In 1936, Captain Charles Orde Wingate, an authority on Arab affairs in the British Intelligence Division, arrived in Palestine. He began to sympathize with the Jewish cause and organized groups of commandos known as Special Night Squads, training them to attack at night, using the tactics of surprise, hit-and-run, and speed.

Wingate had learned Arabic, but now he studied Hebrew and became deeply attached to the Holy Land and the new settlements in Palestine, especially Degania. When asked what he knew about Zionism, he answered that there was only one important book on the subject, the Bible, and he had read that thoroughly. In fact, he could recite large parts of it by heart in Hebrew.

Dayan joined a group of Wingate's commandos, and the British officer took a great liking to him. Wingate appointed him as his second in command in 1937, when Dayan was only 22. He took part in almost all the actions under Wingate's command and from him learned the swift tactics and bold strategy that he himself put to such good use later. Wingate called Dayan his friend and predicted that he would bring great victories to his people.

Wingate's superiors were not pleased with his friendship with the Jews and his devotion to Zionism, and he was recalled to England. At a farewell party in Jerusalem, he repeated the words of the 137th Psalm, "If I forget thee, O Jerusalem, let my right hand forget her cunning."

He and his wife, Lorna, never forgot Jerusalem, but he never saw it again. Nor did the Jews forget him; they called him *Hayedid*, "The Friend." Some veterans of the Jewish Brigade named their group after him.

During the War of Independence, their settlement was besieged. Lorna Wingate was flown over it in a small plane and dropped into the village the copy of the Bible Wingate always carried on his campaigns. In it she had written an inspiring and encouraging message. The settlers beat back the attackers, as Wingate would have wanted them to do.

During World War II, as a Brigadier General, Wingate fought in Ethiopia against the Italians, and in Burma, where he died in a plane crash on March 24, 1944, at age 41. Orde Wingate was an unusual man, a British officer devoted to Zionism when so many British politicians were working against it. Like Mickey Marcus later, he turned the Jewish fighters into first-class soldiers. On account of his contributions and influence, he may well be considered a hero of Israel.

In October, 1939, the British authorities cracked down hard on Haganah. They discovered the training school for officers and arrested

43 men, including Allon, Sadeh, Yadin, and Dayan. Tried for illegal activities, such as possession of weapons, they were found guilty and sentenced to long terms of imprisonment at Acre.

Dayan became the leader of the Jewish prisoners. He also kept busy improving his knowledge of Arabic and reading political works. After 16 months, the Haganah prisoners were released because the British needed their help in World War II. Dayan took part in the same Syrian campaign in which Allon had participated, but Dayan's unit went by way of Lebanon.

Dayan led his men ahead of Australian troops on June 8, 1941. He was asked to go 12 miles across the border, capture a fort, and wait for the Australians to arrive. Using Wingate's tactics of surprise, Dayan had his men storm the building and overpower the guard. Later, he went up on the roof to look over the countryside. The enemy were making a counterattack, and a bullet struck his field glasses.

Zalman Mart, one of his men, rushed to give first aid. Dayan's left eye was gone, and blood was streaming down his cheek, but he remained calm. In the spirit of Trumpeldor, he ordered his men not to bother with him but to keep the enemy busy. Years later, Mart praised Dayan's bravery on this occasion, saying, "I shall never forget the courage he showed at that time. He certainly behaved like a hero."

After the Australians arrived, and the enemy were beaten off, Dayan was placed on a truck and taken to a hospital in Haifa. When he came out of it, he was wearing a black patch over the place where his left eye had been. Later that year, he went to live in Jerusalem with his wife and daughter, Yael, who was born in 1939. She is now a writer.

During the rest of the war Dayan helped set up a radio network in Palestine and form sabotage units. He also suggested to the British that they form parachute units of Jewish volunteers to work behind the Nazi lines in occupied countries. The British did not follow his suggestion until a few years later. Hannah Senesh was among those volunteers. At the end of the war, Dayan returned to Nahalal and became a farmer again but remained in the reserve corps of Haganah as a lieutenant colonel.

When the War of Independence broke out in 1948, Itzhak Sadeh asked him to form a commando unit, the 89th Battalion. He took part in the campaign to capture Ramla and Lod (Lydda), towns that threatened the approach to Tel Aviv. His aggressive tactics, as he stormed through Lydda with a column of jeeps, prepared the way for the capture of Lydda and Ramla a few days later.

Lieutenant Colonel Natanel Lorch of the Israel Defense Forces has called Dayan's raid on Lydda "one of the most daring operations undertaken during the War of Independence."

On the very next day, July 13, 1948, orders were received from Yigael Yadin, Chief of Staff of Haganah, to go to the Negev, then occupied by the Egyptians. After a day of preparations, the 89th Battalion set out to relieve the kibbutz of Negba, which was being besieged, and to seize Caratia (Kharatya) in order to open the road to the Negev. Dayan's battle-weary troops took Caratia on July 18 after a night battle.

On July 23, Ben-Gurion appointed Dayan commander of the New City of Jerusalem. In spite of a truce declared on July 18, the Arabs were attacking from the Old City, and fighting was going on in other parts of Israel. Dayan took an active part in some of these clashes.

Later, he secretly crossed into Jordan a few times for discussions with King Abdullah and attended meetings on the island of Rhodes that finally brought an armistice. As the chief military delegate for Israel, he signed the agreement with Jordan in April, 1949.

Although Dayan was only 35 in 1950, he had performed military duties for more than 20 years. He might have wanted to go back to working on his farm and spending more time with his family. In addition to the one daughter, Yael, there were now two sons, Ehud, who became a farmer, and Assaf, now known as an actor. However, Dayan remained in military service and was promoted to the rank of Brigadier General.

In 1952, he went to England to study at the Senior Officers' School, and after his return, he became Deputy Chief of Staff of the Israel Defense Forces. In 1953, Dayan was one of the Israeli representatives at a meeting of the Security Council of the United Nations to discuss the Israeli-Jordan border dispute.

He was called home to become Chief of Staff on December 1 and was named a Major General, the highest rank of general in the Israel Defense Forces. He insisted on strict training, physical fitness, and aggressiveness. All officers had to take commando or paratroop training. Since he did not ask others to do what he himself would not do, he learned how to parachute.

War with Egypt and Jordan was drawing closer. Arab terrorist bands were planting mines, destroying property, shooting at villagers, and killing farmers. Arabs in the Old City fired into the New City.

In return, Dayan sent commando units to counterattack and to capture positions held by the Egyptians and Jordanians. He set an example of bravery to his men. In some of the clashes, Dayan went to the front of the troops, calling upon them to follow him, even though they begged him not to endanger his life.

"Follow me!" and not "Forward!" was the command he gave, and his officers followed his example. The number of casualties among Israeli officers was high because they fought alongside their men.

When France and Great Britain were angered by Nasser's seizure of the Suez Canal, Dayan, who had received the award of the French Legion of Honor in 1954, flew to Paris to discuss a plan of action and to obtain aircraft, ammunition, and tanks. He impressed General Bernard Challe, French Deputy Air Chief, by his clear analysis and confident manner. When asked by General Paul Ely, French Chief of Staff, how long he thought it would take the Israelis to reach the Suez Canal, Dayan is said to have replied, "That depends on how fast the vehicles you give us are." France promised to send all necessary equipment and arms.

The war broke out on October 29, 1956. Dayan's plan of action called for speed and surprise. The Egyptians looked for an attack in the Sinai peninsula along the usual route from the north, but the Israelis' main attack was made in the desert region of the south. The soldiers advanced so rapidly that they covered about 200 miles through the sand and captured the strategic position of Sharm el Sheikh on the Straits of Tiran, thereby guaranteeing freedom of shipping for Israel to and from Eilat.

Colonel Avraham Yoffe, a hardy, stocky veteran "built like a tank," was in command of the 9th Brigade, known as Gideon's Battalion, consisting of reservists, mainly farmers, in this campaign in the desert. His leadership and the speed with which he moved his tanks over sand dunes won fame for him in military history and a place among Israel's heroes.

Upon retirement from the armed forces, he engaged in nature conservation for the state. In 1967, he was back in service, and as Brigadier General Yoffe he commanded a division – once again in the Sinai! Two other Brigadier Generals, Yisrael Tal and Ariel Sharon, fought in the Sinai both in 1956 and in 1967!

In an interview, Yoffe said, "I want to point out that all my division, from the Commander down are civilians and were civilians up to three weeks ago....This is the common thing in Israel where today you are a soldier and the next day something else."

Or, as Kishon has written, "It is a country where every human being is a soldier, and every soldier is a human being." Girls fought heroically in the Haganah and other underground groups. Today, unmarried women between ages 18-26 are drafted into the Israel

Moshe Dayan

Defense Forces. They perform valuable noncombatant services and have received great praise for their work and contribution to the morale of the fighting men.

In the 1956 war, Dayan visited almost every scene of the fighting, often taking charge where the action was not going well. He exposed himself to danger, flying low over the battlefields. He made a dramatic visit to Colonel Yoffe, conversing with him from the air and giving encouragement. At one time, Dayan narrowly escaped death when his small plane was shot at, and at another time, he was almost hit by a sniper.

Within a week, all major points had been taken by the Israeli armies, from El Arish in the northeastern part of the Sinai peninsula to Sharm el Sheikh in the south. Such was the speed of the Israeli victory that Sharm el Sheikh was captured on November 5, the day on which the French and British first entered the action by dropping paratroopers on Port Said. A cease-fire came the next day.

The Sinai War established Dayan as a military leader whose fame spread to other countries. He wrote a book called *Diary of the Sinai Campaign*, which was studied by officers in staff colleges.

After this war, Dayan traveled on commercial and diplomatic missions, usually with Shimon Peres, a loyal follower of Ben-Gurion and an active worker in the Defense Ministry, to West Germany, Africa, and Asia. At the end of 1957, he took a leave from the army to resume his studies, which he had never been able to complete because of his services to the state. At age 42, he entered the Tel Aviv School of Law and Economics, resigned as Chief of Staff, and gave full attention to his work at the school, from which he received the degree of Bachelor of Science. He also studied political science at the Hebrew University.

Dayan then began to interest himself in politics. He also became a goodwill ambassador of Israel, appearing at rallies and meetings, and on radio and TV in the United States and Europe. In Israel, he worked for Ben-Gurion's Mapai party. In 1959, Dayan was appointed Minister of Agriculture. He tried to modernize methods and to have the farmers grow produce for export. Organization was his keyword.

After Ben-Gurion had resigned as Premier in 1963, Dayan did not get along well with his successor, Levi Eshkol. After a short time, he got out of politics.

He became the manager of a fishing company. He also gave time to his hobby, archeology, in which he had become interested during a campaign when he was attracted by some shells and objects of ancient times. As he developed this hobby, he toured around the country in search of pieces for his collection.

He became a correspondent for a Tel Aviv newspaper, receiving an assignment to cover the Vietnam war in March, 1966. During his frequent absences, his son, Ehud, took care of the farm at Nahalal. Dayan's wife, Ruth, became a leader in Israel's fashion industry.

When he saw how tense the situation between the Arabs and Israel had become, Dayan spoke out strongly. He expressed the view that President Nasser of Egypt was the real enemy and that Israel had to be tougher. The people also thought that Eshkol was not firm enough toward Nasser, and even many of Dayan's political opponents wanted him to be the Minister of Defense at this critical time.

Overcome by rising public pressure, Eshkol, who together with Golda Meir, favored Allon, gave in to the wishes of the people. On June 1, 1967, Dayan became Minister of Defense. War broke out on the 5th; some authorities believe that one of the causes was a false report spread by the Russians that Israel was gathering troops for an attack against Syria.

On the 7th, Israel had attained most of her objectives. The Israelis destroyed almost all the Egyptian planes, defeated Egypt's armies, took a vast number of supplies, vehicles, and prisoners, and occupied the Gaza Strip and Sinai, reaching the Suez Canal.

When Jordan entered the war, she was also disastrously defeated, and Israel captured the Old City of Jerusalem. Dayan was very moved when he stood at the Wailing Wall; he declared, "We have returned to Jerusalem never to part from her again."

Syria entered the ground fighting on the 6th; her planes, like those of Egypt and Jordan, had been put out of action. The Israelis drove the Syrians back and captured the Golan Heights, from which the Syrians used to shell Israeli settlements.

The war, known as the Six-Day War, came to an end on June 10 through a cease-fire arranged by the United Nations, but there was no peace between Israel and the Arab nations. The Arabs' declared policy was, "No peace, no negotiations, and no recognition." Abba Eban has said, "It was the only war in history when the victor sued for peace and the vanquished called for unconditional surrender." Nasser called off the cease-fire for Egypt on April 23, 1969. Under these conditions, Israel has held on to the occupied territory while waiting for the Arabs to agree to negotiate terms of peace.

Dayan emerged from the war as a glamorous leader. Eshkol gave credit to the plans made by Major General Itzhak Rabin, then Chief of Staff, and others before the war broke out. Dayan acknowledged the part played by Rabin, but he added plans of his own and was responsible for the speed with which they were carried out. Above all,

Itzhak Rabin

he provided the personal leadership, drive, and imagination.

Itzhak Rabin is one of the heroes of Israel. He is a sabra who was born in Jerusalem in 1922. He fought in the Syrian campaign in which Dayan and Allon had taken part, and like them, was a leader in the War of Independence. In 1968, he was appointed Ambassador to the United States.

Rabin's place as Chief of Staff was taken by Major General Chaim Bar-Lev, who represents the new type of Israeli military leaders, those not trained by the British. The frequent changes of leaders of the armed forces show that there is no military establishment in Israel. The commanders serve when they are needed and then go back into civilian life or take up a political or diplomatic career.

There are many other military heroes of Israel, only a few of whom can be mentioned briefly. Major General Chaim Herzog, now retired, contributed greatly to the development of Israel's superb intelligence service. Major General Mordechai Hod is the Commander in Chief of Israel's excellent air force. During the 1967 War, Brigadier (now Major) General Yeshayahu Gavish was the commander of the southern forces in Sinai.

Another great leader in that campaign was Brigadier (also now Major) General Yisrael Tal, like Gavish, little known here. He won the 1961 Israel Security Prize for "weapon improvement." In Israel he is known as Mr. Armor for his great devotion to tank warfare. General Tal is a master of desert fighting and has helped develop what is considered the world's most effective tank corps.

Such are some of the leaders with whom Moshe Dayan, as Minister of Defense, has worked and is working — a first-rate, dedicated team!

Of his own private life, Dayan has said, "I prefer to go off somewhere by myself, if I have the time." In the last few years he certainly has not had the time. Many persons think of him as a candidate for the position of Premier some day, but he has been too occupied with directing the stepped-up undeclared war between Egypt (now called the United Arab Republic) and Syria to think of politics. In addition, the Israelis have to fight against the fedayeen, guerrilla and commando bands, whose largest group is Al Fatah, and Arab Palestinian nationalist and liberation groups.

Lebanon did not take part in the 1967 War, and the cease-fire ending that war is still in effect between Jordan and Israel. However, the commando groups take refuge in these countries and make raids or fire upon Israeli frontier settlements. The governments of Lebanon and Jordan are unable to control the guerrillas; Syria, of course, is unwilling to stop them.

Russian help to Arab countries, especially to Egypt, increased tremendously after the 1967 War. Planes, tanks, ammunition, and the latest and most powerful kinds of anti-aircraft missiles were given to Egypt. Russian soldiers, advisers, technicians, and pilots came to Egypt.

Arab raids were met with force, and Israeli troops made counterattacks. Fighting along the Suez Canal became intense. Up to August 7, 1970, air strikes were made by Israeli planes for more than 70 days in a row to hit missile sites in Egypt and to keep the Egyptians from making full-scale war.

So serious had the situation become because of the Russians' help to the Arabs that one Israeli official said, "Our secret weapon used to be the A.B. — Ayn Brera. Now it is the A.B.C. — Ayn Brera Clal — No Choice, Alternative, or Remedy Whatsoever." The Israelis felt that they had nowhere to go and no choice except to fight on — that was their moral weapon.

The entrance of the Soviet Union into the Middle East presented a serious problem to that country also and to the United States. There was the danger of a clash between the two great powers over their interests in the Middle East. Therefore, on June 19, 1970, the United States made public a peace proposal to be negotiated by Egypt, Jordan, Syria, and Israel, as the countries most directly concerned.

This was similar to a resolution of the United Nations of November 22, 1967. The United States plan called for negotiations concerning recognition of Israel's right to exist as a nation, her withdrawal from occupied territory, and freedom of navigation in the Suez Canal and the Straits of Tiran. Negotiations were to begin during a 90-day cease-fire period; Dr. Gunnar V. Jarring, as special representative of the United Nations, would act as a mediator, or go-between.

Nasser accepted the United States proposal. It is believed that he was persuaded by the Russians, who feared that the situation was getting to be too dangerous. Receiving a pledge about her security from the United States, Israel also accepted. Other Arab states, with the exception of Syria, Iraq, Algeria, and South Yemen, followed Nasser's lead. Most of the guerrillas, however, refused to stop fighting. On August 7, 1970, the cease-fire went into effect, and all was quiet on the Suez front.

As Minister of Defense, Moshe Dayan found little time during the fighting for leisure activities like archeology, his favorite hobby. Even during the cease-fire he still had to make plans to meet the attacks of the guerrillas and to watch the activities of the Arab nations that had not agreed to the cease-fire. He also had to be prepared for any sudden turn of events, and, like other government officials, he was concerned with the problem of the Arabs in Israel and in the occupied territories.

A final story about one of his archeological expeditions shows the character of the man. While he was digging on March 20, 1968, a cave-in buried him under a mound of earth. As he tells the story, "I told myself that this time this was it. I saw the hill slide and I knew that I couldn't get out."

Children looking on spread the alarm, and Dayan was dug out. His first words were an inquiry about the safety of a young man who had been digging with him. Rushed to a hospital, Dayan did not show any emotion, although the doctors could see that he was in great pain. First, he asked for a telephone because he had to make important calls about actions being taken against Al Fatah raiders from Syria.

Only then did he allow the doctors to look after him. Later, when asked about Dayan, the head of the hospital answered, "He behaved like a hero," and then added, "just like Moshe Dayan."

Abraham Yoffe

Yisrael Tal

Golda Meir

Israel's First Lady Premier

On May 10, 1948, an automobile with a woman and a man in it, crossed from the Jewish part of Palestine into Transjordan. The woman was dressed in Arab costume, a flowing gown and a long veil. She was Golda Myerson, later known as Golda Meir, going on a secret mission to meet King Abdullah of Transjordan, who had agreed to wait for her in the house of one of his faithful friends. The object of her mission was to persuade the King to have his country live in peace with the State of Israel that would soon arise.

It was a dangerous mission for all of them. Golda Myerson and her companion, Ezra Dinnan, her interpreter and an expert on Arab affairs, had to ride through hostile territory patrolled by armed bands. The other Arab chiefs did not want peace with the Jews; in fact, Abdullah was assassinated in 1951 for being too friendly with them. On the very day of the meeting, Iraqi troops had gathered near the border, ready to invade Israel.

Under these circumstances, King Abdullah was unable to come to a friendly agreement as long as the Jews would not give up the idea of building their state. Somehow, Mrs. Myerson and Dinnan got back safely across the border.

Golda Meir, as we shall now call her, was born on May 3, 1898, in Kiev, Russia, one of eight children, only three of whom lived beyond childhood. Her father, Moshe Mabovitch, was a carpenter who decided to leave for the United States in 1903 because of anti-Semitism and pogroms. The family remained in Russia until he could earn enough money to send for them. After a short stay in New York, he went to Milwaukee, Wisconsin, and three years later, the family joined him. They were so poor that they had to live first in one room, and then in two small rooms in back of a store. The mother added a little to the family income by selling groceries in the store while the father went out to work as a carpenter.

In 1906, Golda entered the Fourth Street School, a public elementary school that is still standing. The school records show that she received high marks in arithmetic, reading, spelling, and German during the seventh year. (German was required because of the large German population in Milwaukee.) She was skipped into the eighth grade after the first half of the seventh. School pictures show that she was tall and good-looking.

She showed her skill as an organizer when she was very young. At age 10, she formed the American Young Sisters' Society, which collected pennies for schoolbooks for the poor. She earned money while attending high school by giving English lessons to immigrants at 10 cents a lesson and by working part-time in a library.

After graduating from high school, she entered the Milwaukee Normal School, a training school for those preparing to teach. She did not finish the course and went to work in a library. However, she did teach later, not in public schools, but in Yiddish folk schools.

Golda had not continued at the Normal School because another interest entered her life, one that has filled her life from that time on. She became an enthusiastic Zionist, and her greatest desire was to get to Palestine. In 1915, at age 17, she joined the Workers of Zion. She became an effective speaker, addressing groups, especially young persons, in English and Yiddish. She also listened to other speakers and was thrilled to hear Ben-Gurion and Ben-Zvi when they came to Milwaukee.

On December 24, 1917, she married Morris Myerson. He was not a Zionist and had to promise to go to Palestine before she would marry him. In the meantime, Golda kept up her Zionist activities. She was a delegate at an American Zionist Congress in Philadelphia and traveled to other cities, speaking and raising money for the Workers of Zion.

Finally, on May 23, 1921, Golda, Morris, her older sister, Shana, and two friends were part of a group that boarded the steamer *Pocahontas* at New York, bound for Naples. From there, after a rough voyage and many hardships, they came to Tel Aviv on July 14.

In a brief visit to Milwaukee on October 3, 1969, Golda Meir, then Prime Minister of Israel, spoke to the pupils of her old elementary school and gave them the reasons for her decision made about 50 years before. She said that until she had come from Russia to Milwaukee she had known only the sufferings of Jews in Eastern Europe, and she added:

"Here I found freedom, kindness, and cleanliness. Later, I learned from my Zionist friends that through our own efforts we could build for the Jewish people a home of our own."

From Tel Aviv she and Morris went to the kibbutz of Merhavia. She worked in the field and in the kitchen, took care of babies, and was selected to take a course in raising poultry. In 1923, she and Morris left the kibbutz and went to live first in Tel Aviv and then in Jerusalem. They had two children, a boy and a girl. From 1924 to 1928, she and her husband led a hard life doing all kinds of work while they were bringing up two small children.

In 1928 she returned to Zionist work. She became secretary of the Women's Labor Council at the request of Histadrut. For the next six years she traveled back and forth between Palestine and London, the United States, and other places. She remained in the United States with her children between 1932 and 1934, working with the Pioneer Women's Organization of America. Ben-Gurion and other Zionist leaders began to hear about her abilities and to recognize her as a coming force in the Zionist movement.

In 1934, she was appointed a member of the Executive of Histadrut and a year later became its secretary. She was now called upon to carry out important programs of Histadrut, travel to the United States, and attend Zionist conferences. She soon became known as one of the outstanding figures of the Jewish labor movement in Palestine.

In July, 1946, the British arrested Jewish leaders, including Moshe Sharett, head of the political department of the Jewish Agency. Since Ben-Gurion was then in Paris, Golda Meir was chosen as the best qualified to become acting head of the Agency. The British knew her well from conferences when they had discussed health and labor conditions with her as a Histadrut leader.

Although she did not favor terrorism, she supported opposition to British policy. She was often questioned by British authorities, including Sir Alan Gordon Cunningham, the High Commissioner. She spoke up without fear, and the British learned to respect her ability and courage.

One story shows what they thought of her. She was stopped by British soldiers while she was on a dangerous mission, and her car was searched for weapons. When the British captain saw her papers, he said to a soldier, "I think we have bitten off more than we can chew!" She and her companion were taken to a police station, given a New Year's Eve party, and were escorted back to Tel Aviv!

Golda Meir undertook many dangerous missions during this period. Haganah leaders consulted her about military policy. Her message of inspiration was, "We must fight, for we have no other way."

She worked to get immigrants into Palestine in defiance of the British ban. Refugees from the *Exodus* were helped to escape from the British zone in Germany.

Golda herself went to Cyprus, where the British were keeping more than 50,000 refugees in camps. There she arranged to have families with small children leave immediately for Palestine.

Early in 1948, she went on an important mission to the United States, where she raised $50,000,000 that the Jews in Palestine needed for buying military equipment against the expected Arab attacks. Ben-Gurion paid Golda Meir this compliment, "Someday it will be written in history that there was a Jewish woman who got the money that made the state possible."

A few days after Golda's meeting with King Abdullah, the State of

Golda Meir

Israel was declared. She is a signer of Israel's Declaration of Independence, on which her name appears as Golda Myerson; she did not change her last name to *Meir* until 1956, five years after her husband died. Soon after Israel was established, Golda was again asked to go to the United States to raise money. While there, she received word that she had been appointed the Israeli Minister to the Soviet Union.

She served in Moscow until early in 1949. After the first election in Israel, as a leading member of Mapai, she entered the Cabinet as Minister of Labor. She provided work and housing for immigrants and built new roads, which the people called "Golden Ways," in her honor. Her slogans were: "Ration clothes, not immigration," and, "Build, create new things."

Golda Meir faced enormous difficulties with her usual vigor and determination. Thousands of immigrants had to be taken into a kind of life that was new to most of them. Money was needed, and once more Golda went on fund-raising campaigns in the United States.

In 1956, she replaced Moshe Sharett as Minister of Foreign Affairs. She often spoke before the United Nations, presenting Israel's case with eloquence after the Sinai War. In 1958, she began a long series of trips to gain friendship for Israel, especially among the new nations of Africa. Israel has sent engineers, technicians, and workers as a kind of unofficial peace corps to help those countries as well as Cambodia and Latin America. In addition, Golda Meir visited Scandinavia, Mexico, and some countries in South America and Asia to establish goodwill.

Abba Eban succeeded Golda Meir as Foreign Minister in 1966. Born in South Africa, February 2, 1915, Eban is different from other Israeli diplomats and political leaders. He was educated at Cambridge University, England, and speaks with a "British university accent." He was a British army officer in Palestine and settled there after World War II. A brilliant orator with the gift of giving voice to memorable phrases and sentences, he has often been heard at meetings of the United Nations and on TV and radio.

After Eban succeeded her, Golda Meir devoted herself to her duties as Secretary General of Mapai. Shortly after the death of Prime Minister Levi Eshkol in March, 1968, she became Prime Minister, or Premier, and retained that position after the election in October, 1969.

Golda Meir makes a strong impression. Speaking firmly and to the point, possessing independence of mind, she commands respect in the field of national and international politics, a remarkable woman in her 70's and a grandmother in an arena dominated by men.

Like a modern Deborah, she was chosen to lead her state, and her

Abba Eban

long and distinguished career of service during such dangerous times has given her a place of honor in the history of Israel.

In his *Aeneid,* the Roman poet Vergil wrote, "So great a task it was to found the Roman state." An Israeli poet could say the same about the Israeli state. Golda Meir is one of the many who dedicated themselves to the difficult task of founding the State of Israel, who gave up almost everything else in life to work for that state.

Now, as its head, Golda Meir works even harder to keep it alive.

Old City and New City, Jerusalem

13

Shmuel Yosef Agnon
Israel's Nobel Prize Winner

Near a small house in Talpiot, a section of Jerusalem, this sign was once placed by order of Mayor Teddy Kollek:

QUIET. AGNON IS WRITING.

Agnon said about the sign, "I should have gained fame because of my stories and in the end I became known because of this sign."

However, Agnon did become famous throughout the world, and not because of the sign, but because of his writing, when he received the Nobel Prize for Literature in 1966. He shared this award with another Jewish writer, the German-born Nelly Sachs, a poet and dramatist who had escaped from Nazi Germany and made her home in Sweden. When she was notified of her award, she remarked, "Agnon represents the State of Israel, I represent the tragedy of the Jewish people." By coincidence, Miss Sachs, who was born on December 10, 1891, died only a few months after Agnon—on May 12, 1970.

Shmuel Yosef Agnon was born on July 17, 1888, in Galicia, Poland. *Agnon* is a pen name that he used since 1909 instead of his real name, *Czaczkes*. His father, a fur merchant, was a Talmudic scholar, and his mother, the daughter of a learned man, was devoted to literature.

Shmuel went to a *heder* (Hebrew elementary school) and to a Baron de Hirsch school. He continued his Hebrew studies with his father and a local rabbi, and soon became interested in Zionism. Through his father, he also became interested in the religious group known as Hasidim, who are given over to mysticism, great zeal, joy, and dancing. Later, he studied the wisdom of the past as well as modern Hebrew and European literature.

Agnon began to write poetry when very young. At age 15, he had some of his Hebrew and Yiddish poems published in newspapers. He continued to write poems and stories that appeared in print. When he was 18, he went to the city of Lvov to work on a newspaper. His love of Zionism was so strong that two years later, in 1908, he left for Palestine. In Jaffa he worked as secretary in a Jewish court, for the Jewish Community Council, and for the Committee of the Lovers of Zion.

Moving to Jerusalem in 1910, he returned to writing. In 1912, he went to Berlin to continue his literary studies. There he earned his living by giving private Hebrew lessons, working as a research assistant, and lecturing on Hebrew literature.

He met Martin Buber (1878-1965), who was very interested in the Hasidim, about whose teachings and ideas he later wrote books. Agnon

Shmuel Yosef Agnon

worked with him, collecting stories of the Hasidim. Buber, who won international fame as a philosopher, author, and scholar, later settled in Israel; he became one of her famous men.

Agnon was unable to leave Germany during World War I. Although the war ended in 1918, he stayed on until 1924. He met a wealthy man, Salman Schocken, who helped him financially, and even started a publishing company, partly to put out Agnon's books. Plans are under way to publish all of Agnon's works in English translations; several have appeared to date.

In about 1929, Agnon built his own house in Talpiot, then a quiet place away from the noise of town. Agnon chose it because he wanted to live and write in peace, but the world around him changed. Kollek had the sign put up because the noise of building might disturb Agnon's quiet.

Greater changes had taken place in Agnon's world much further away and many years before. In 1932, Agnon went back to Poland to visit the scenes of his childhood. He was very unhappy at what he saw there. Life had changed in the Jewish communities. In many stories, Agnon writes with deep feeling about the loss of the old way of life. In 1937, he wrote a novel, translated into English under the title *A Guest for the Night.* In it he tells about a man who returns after a long absence to his old *shtetl,* or village. The man is very sad about the complete change he sees; the book really tells how Agnon himself must have felt.

The world of his readers had also changed. Many of them were gone—they were among the 6,000,000 killed by Hitler's Nazis. However, Agnon had admirers of his works, especially among critics. One of them, an American, Edmund Wilson, nominated him for the Nobel Prize. The Committee that selected the winners said in its announcement that one of Agnon's novels, *The Bridal Canopy,* is in "its ingenious and earthy humor a Jewish counterpart of *Don Quixote.*"

The Bridal Canopy, which has been translated from Hebrew into English, is the story of a poor Hasid, Reb Yudel, who has three daughters. It is time for them to get married, but he and his wife have no money for the dowries, wedding gifts to be given to the men who will be picked as their husbands. Accompanied by a wagoner, Reb Nuta, Reb Yudel wanders over the countryside to beg or, in some other honest way, get enough money for the dowries.

The two men meet all kinds of persons, entertain and are entertained. Throughout there are reflections on life, displays of learning, imagination, and wisdom, together with stories and earthy talk by Reb Nuta. Ben Yudel and his wife are able to give the dowries, see their daughters happily married, and can look forward to a joyful old age.

Agnon twice won the highest award Israel can give to an author, the Bialik Prize of the City of Tel Aviv. In 1967, he visited the United States to receive honorary degrees from Columbia, Yeshiva University, and the Jewish Theological Seminary.

He died on February 17, 1970, at age 82. He is survived by his widow, the former Esther Marx, whom he married in 1919, a son, a daughter, and five grandchildren. He was honored with a state funeral.

Agnon found inspiration in the Bible, the wise men of old, and the mystic stories of the Hasidim. Although his way of writing belongs to the past, it is also part of the present. His stories are human, with a meaning that is not bounded by time.

So, this book ends with a chapter about a man of peace. In an interview taped shortly before his death and shown as a memorial to him on February 22, 1970, Agnon said about the people of Israel:

"They did not want to conquer; they wanted to defend themselves and save their lives."

Many of the chapters of this book are about heroes of war. Circumstances and history have compelled the Israelis to defend themselves to keep themselves and their country alive. More is therefore heard about the military activities of Israel every day; too little is heard about her wonderful cultural achievements.

With a population only about one-third that of New York City, Israel has in a very short time accomplished more in architecture, arts and crafts, literature, music and dance, painting and sculpture, the theater and film, and scholarship and education than many large countries. In addition to the names mentioned elsewhere in this book, we may call to mind the Israeli Philharmonic Orchestra, the singers Shoshanna Damari and Geula Gil, the composer Paul Ben-Haim, the Inbal (Yemenite dance group) and Batsheva Dancers, Habimah, the National Theater performing in Hebrew, and its great actress, Hanna Rovina, and other more modern repertory theaters, the artist Reuven Rubin, and the art colonies of Safed, Ein Hod (near Haifa), and the Old City of Jaffa.

It has been said that next to oranges, musicians are the chief export of Israel. To mention only a few—there are the pianists David Bar-Illan, Daniel Barenboim, and Joseph Kalichstein, and the violinists Itzhak Perlman and Pinchas Zukerman.

The Israelis would much rather be heroes of peace engaged in cultural activities, in scientific research, in improving their land, than in being called from the enjoyment of peace to the horrors of war—even if war turns them into heroes.

Actually, life in Israel calls for heroism by Israelis of every age. They all long, however, for the day when the words will come true which their prophet Isaiah spoke and which are cut into a wall near the building of the United Nations:

> *They shall beat their swords into plowshares, and their swords into pruninghooks; nations shall not lift up sword against nation, neither shall they learn war any more.*

This is the message to the world of the heroes and heroines of Israel, the land of the People of the Book.

Shalom, "Peace."

Inscription opposite United Nations Building, New York

Index

Aaronson, Aaron, 33, 72
Aaronson, Sarah, 72, 73
Abdullah, King, 90, 112, 114
Abraham, 9
Agnon, Shmuel Yosef, 119-123
Ahad Ha'am, 18, 64
Akiba, Rabbi, 12
Alexander the Great, 11
Alexandria, 11, 42, 57
Al Fatah, 109, 111
Aliyah, 18, 70
Allenby, General Edmund, 30, 43
Allon, Yigal, 80, 83, 88, 94-99, 100, 102
Altalena, 49
Antiochus IV Epiphanes, 11, 12
anti-Semitism, 21, 22, 55, 112
Aqaba, Gulf of, 52, 54, 90
Arabic, 41, 68, 71, 94, 99, 101, 102
Arabs, 16, 35, 36, 43, 44, 45, 48, 49, 50, 60, 84, 94, 99, 107, 110
Aramaic, 68, 69
Ashkenazim, 62
Assyrians, 10
Australians, 96, 102
Auto-Emancipation, 13, 25
Ayn Brera (ein breira), 82, 110

Babylonian Captivity, or Exile, 10, 11
Balfour, Lord Alfred, 31, 32, 33
Balfour Declaration, 33
Barenboim, Daniel, 122
Bar Giora, 12, 41
Bar-Illan, David, 122
Bar Kochba, Simon, 12, 15, 90
Bar-Lev, General Chaim, 109
Basle Congress and Program, 26
Bedouins, 16, 91, 100
Begin, Menahem, 46, 49, 50
Ben-Gurion, David, 26, 29, 37, 39-54, 57, 80, 82, 83, 84, 88, 90, 92, 97, 106, 113, 114
Ben-Gurion, Paula, 42, 51, 54, 114
Ben Yehuda, Deborah, 63, 64, 65
Ben Yehuda, Eliezer, 62-71

Ben Yehuda, Hemda, 65, 67, 68, 70, 71
Ben-Zvi, Itzhak, 41, 42, 51, 57, 113
Bernadotte, Count Folke, 49
Bethlehem, 48, 90, 91
Bevin, Ernest, 46, 48
Bezalel Museum, 70
Bialik, Chaim Nachman, 64
Bialik Prize, 122
Bible, 50, 54, 64, 88, 90, 96
Biltmore Program, 46
Bilu, Biluim, 15, 16, 18, 62, 64
Bridal Canopy, The, 121-122
British, 35, 42-46, 48, 72, 88, 97, 101, 102, 114
Buber, Martin, 119-120
Budapest, 19, 72, 73, 75
Bunche, Dr. Ralph, 49
"Burma Road" of Israel, 83

Canaan, 9
Carmi, Israel, 80
cease-fire: of 1948, 49, 84; of 1956, 52, 106; of 1967, 107; of 1970, 110
chalutzim (pioneers), 16, 58
Chorev, Amos, 83
Churchill, Winston, 32, 46
"City of Slaughter," 64
Claude's Wife, 15
concentration camps, 78-80
Constantinople, 26, 42, 65, 67
Coptic, 70
Cyprus, 27, 114
Cyrus the Great, 11

Daniel, 9
Daniel Deronda, 15
Daniel Sieff Research Institute, 35
Daphne, Reuben, 73, 75
David, King, 9, 54, 84
Dayan, Moshe, 80, 84, 90, 93, 96, 100-111
Dayan, Ruth, 100, 107
Dead Sea Scrolls, 90-93
Deborah, 9, 96, 116

125

Declaration of Independence of Israel, 48, 50, 82, 116
Deer, The (Hatzevi), 63, 64, 65, 68
Degania, 57, 100, 101
Diary of the Sinai Campaign, 106
Diaspora, 10, 12
Don Quixote, 82; the book, 121
Dori, Yaakov, 80, 97
Dreschler, Deborah, 60
Dreyfus, Captain Alfred, 19, 22
Dühring, Karl Eugen, 21, 22
Dumas, Alexandre, 15

Eban, Abba, 37, 82, 107, 116
Egypt, 9, 11, 49, 51, 52, 73, 99, 103, 107, 110
Eilat (Elath), 90, 104
ein breira (Ayn Brera), 82, 110
Eleazar, the Zealot, 86
Elijah, 9
Eliot, George, 15
Eshkol, Levi, 99, 106, 107, 116
Esther, Queen, 9
Exodus 1947, 46, 114
Ezekiel, 9

fedayeen, 109
Feisal, Emir, 33
France, 22, 52, 104

Galilee, 41, 57, 58, 72, 97
Gavish, General Yeshayahu, 109
Gaza Strip, 52, 107
Germans, 45, 72, 73
Germany, 31, 35, 44, 77, 114, 121
Gideon, 9, 58, 96
Gil, Geula, 122
Glubb Pasha, 82
Golan Heights, 107
Golomb, Eliahu, 43
Gordon, Aaron David, 57
Grand Duke of Baden, 25, 26
Grand Mufti of Jerusalem, 43, 44
Great Britain, 35, 36, 45, 48, 52, 104
Green, Avigdor, 39

Habima, 122
Hadassah, 35
Haganah, 41, 43, 46, 50, 88, 96, 100, 101, 114
Haifa, 17, 97
Halevi, Judah ben Samuel, 64
Hamburger, Jossi, 84
Hanukah, 11
Hashahar ("The Dawn"), 13, 63
Hashomer, 41, 61
Hasid, Hasidim, 119, 120, 121
Hatikvah, 48
Hebrew language, 18, 39, 41, 62-65, 68, 70-71, 72, 80, 101, 119
Hebrews, 9

Hebrew University (Jerusalem), 30, 33, 88, 90, 91
Hechler, Reverend William, 24, 25
Herod the Great, 11, 12, 86, 88
Herzl, Theodor, 18, 19-29, 30, 31, 39, 63, 67, 68, 70, 75
Herzog, General Chaim, 80, 109
Hess, Moses, 25
Hilldring, General John H., 78
Hirsch, Baron Moritz, 16, 22, 24
Histadrut, 43, 113, 114
Hitler, Adolf, 35, 44, 72, 73, 77, 121
Hod, General Mordechai, 109
Holmes, Sherlock, 70, 91
Hungary, 72, 73

Inbal, 122
Iraq, 49, 50, 110
Irgun, 46, 49
Isaiah, 9, 50, 123
Israel: Kingdom of, 10; Land and State of, 9, 10, 26, 37. 39, 48, 52, 63, 65, 109, 112, 119
Israel Defense Forces (IDF, *Zahal*), 50, 90, 103; women in the, 104-105
Israelis, 49, 107, 109, 122
Israelites, 10, 99

Jabotinsky, Vladimir Ze'ev, 42, 44, 45, 46, 57, 58, 70
Jacob, 10
Jaffa, 10, 39, 41, 119, 122
Jarring, Gunnar V., 110
Jeremiah, 9
Jerusalem, 10, 11, 12, 17, 30, 48, 49, 65, 82, 83, 90, 103, 107, 113, 119
Jewish Agency, 35, 44, 48, 82. 114
Jewish Brigade, 45, 46
Jewish Legion, 42
Jewish State, The, 24-25, 27
Jews, 9, 11, 13, 17, 33, 35, 36, 39, 45, 72
John of Gischala, 12
Johnson, Dr. Samuel, 68
Jordan, 49, 50, 52, 103, 107, 109, 110
Josephus, 86, 88
Joshua, 9, 58
Judah, Kingdom of, 10
Judas Maccabeus, 11, 58
Judea, 10, 11

Katznelson, Berl, 42, 44
Keren Hayesod, 36
Kfar Giladi, 60, 72
Kfar Tabor, 94, 96
kibbutz, 51
Kishinev, pogrom in, 28, 64
Kishon, Ephraim, 9, 104
Knesset, 50, 52

126

Kollek, Mayor Teddy, 119, 121
Ladino, 62
Land of Gilead, 15
Larousse, Pierre, 68
Laskov, Chaim, 80
Lazarus, Emma, 15
Lebanon, 49, 50, 96, 102, 109
Leven, Narcisse, 67
Lion of Judah Monument, 61
London Zionist Conference, 43
Lost Tribes, 10
Lovers of Zion, 15, 18, 119
Lydda (Lod), 102, 103

Mabovitch, Moshe, 112
Maccabees, 11, 15, 25, 65, 82
Magic Carpet, Operation, 50
Mandate, British, 34-35, 37
Mapai, 44, 106, 116
Marcus, Colonel (David) Mickey, 77-85, 101
Marcus, Emma, 77, 78, 80, 82
Marranos, 13
Masada, 86, 88, 90
Mattathias, 11
Meir, Golda, 99, 107, 112-118
Melting Pot, The, 24
Merhavia, 113
Message of the Scrolls, The, 93
Metulla, 60
Mickey Marcus Road, 83
Mikveh Israel, 15
Milwaukee, 112, 113
Montefiore, Sir Moses Haim, 16
Moses, 9, 99
moshav, 100
Mount Herzl, 29, 75
Mount Scopus, 30
Mule Corps, 58
Myerson, Golda, 112, 116
Myerson, Morris, 113, 116

Nahalal, 72, 100, 102, 107
Nasser, Gamal Abdel, 51, 52, 107
Nassi, Joseph, 13, 16
Nazis, 72, 73, 121
Nebuchadnezzar, 10
Negev, 51, 88, 99, 103
Netter, Dr. Charles, 15
New City, 49, 83, 90, 103
New Free Press, 19, 21, 24, 27
New Ghetto, The, 22, 26
Nili, 33
Nobel Prize for Literature, 119, 121
Nordau, Dr. Max, 24, 25, 26, 28, 67
Nussbacker, Joel, 73, 75

Old City, 49, 82, 90, 92, 93, 107
Old New Land (*Altneuland*), 26-27
Old Testament, 9, 13, 64
Oliphant, Laurence, 15

Palestine, 10, 12, 13, 15, 18, 24, 25, 27, 35, 39, 45, 48, 57, 63, 65, 72, 79, 80, 101, 112, 114
Palestine White Paper, 45, 46
Palmach, 50, 82, 96, 97
partisans, 73
Partition Plan of the UN, 48, 49
Passover, 9, 13
Patterson, Colonel John Henry, 58
Peel Report, 45
Peicovitch, Reuben, 94
Peres, Shimon, 106
Petah Tikvah, 39
Pinsker, Dr. Leo, 13, 18, 25
procurators, 11
Promised Land, the, 9
Purim, 9

Qumram, caves of, 91

Rabin, Itzhak, 48, 80, 82, 107-108
Rehovoth, 27, 35, 36, 37
Review, The (*Hashkafah*), 68
Rhodes, 50
Rishon Le Zion, 15, 16, 27, 41, 62
Road of Courage, 83
Romans, 11, 12, 86, 88
Rome and Jerusalem, 25
Rothschild, Baron Edmond de, 15, 16-17, 18, 25, 63, 65, 67, 68
Rothschild, Lord Lionel Walter, 33
Rubin, Reuven, 122
Russia, 16, 31, 39, 52, 55, 107, 110, 112, 113
Russo-Japanese War, 55-56

sabra, 94
Sachs, Nelly, 119
Sadeh, Itzhak, 80, 96, 97, 100, 102
Safed, 17, 97, 122
Samson, 9
Samuel, 9
Samuel, Sir Herbert, 44
Schatz, Boris, 70
Sde Boker, 51, 54
Sdot Yam, 72, 75
Sejera, 41
Senesh, Catherine, Mrs., 73, 75
Senesh, Hannah, 72-76, 102
Sephardic, 62, 96
Shamir, Major Shlomo, 77, 78, 80
Sharett (Shertok), Moshe, 36-37, 42, 48, 51, 52, 82, 114, 116
Sharm el Sheik, 104, 106
Sharon, General Ariel, 104
Sherlock Holmes, 70, 91
Shrine of the Book, 93
shtetl, 121
Sinai, 52, 107

Sinai War (of 1956), 52, 104–106
Six-Day War (1967 War), 52–54, 100, 107
Smolenskin, Peretz, 13, 17, 18, 64
Solomon, 9, 10
Soviet Union (Russia), 52, 110, 116
Stern Gang (*Lehi*), 46, 49
Stone, Mickey (Mickey Marcus), 80, 83
Suez Canal, 52, 104, 107, 110
Sukenik, Eleazar, 88, 90–91, 92, 93
Supernumerary Police, 88, 101
Syria, 49, 50, 52, 96, 107, 109, 110
Szold, Henrietta, 35–36

Tabarin, 21
Tacitus, 12
Tal, General Yisrael, 104
Talpiot, 119, 121
Tel Aviv, 28, 37, 48, 80, 82, 83, 84, 102, 113
Tel Hai, 58, 60, 61
Temple: First (of Solomon), 9, 10, 50, 82; Second, 11, 12, 82, 86; of Herod, 12
Ten Plagues (military operation), 99
"This Is Not the Way," 18
Tiberias, 13, 16, 17
Tiran, Straits of, 52, 54, 104, 110
Titus, 12, 41, 86
Torah, 10, 18
Trever, John C., 92
Truman, President Harry S., 36, 37
Trumpeldor, Joseph, 55–61, 72, 102
Turks, 13, 16, 30, 33, 42, 57, 65, 67, 71, 72
Twelve Tribes, 10, 18

Uganda offer, 28, 31
United Arab Republic (Egypt), 109
United Nations, 24, 36, 48, 49, 52, 90, 103, 107, 110, 116, 123
United States peace proposal, 110
Ussishkin, Menahem Mendel, 64

Vergil, 118
Vespasian, 11, 12, 86
Vichy French, 96

Vienna, 19, 21, 24, 28, 67
Wailing Wall (Western Wall), 12, 107
War of Independence, 49, 61, 75, 88, 90, 101, 102
Webster, Noah, 68
Weizmann, Chaim, 29, 30–38, 39, 43, 45, 71
Weizmann, Michael, 32, 35
Weizmann, Vera, 32, 35, 36
Weizmann Institute of Science, 36, 37
Western Wall (Wailing Wall), 12
West Point, 77, 85
White Papers, 35, 44, 45, 46
Wilbushevitz, Manya, 41
Wilhelm II, Kaiser, 25, 26–27
Wingate, Lorna, 101
Wingate, Orde, 101, 102
Workers of Zion, 39, 41, 42, 113
World War I, 32, 42, 57, 71, 72
World War II, 45, 72, 88, 97, 101
World Zionist Organization, 26, 30, 35, 36, 44, 67

Yadin, Yigael, 80, 82, 83, 86–93, 96, 97, 102, 103
Yemen, Yemenites, 50
Yiddish, 62, 113, 119
Yishuv, 17, 71
Yoffe, General Avraham, 104, 105
Yonas, Deborah, 62, 63
Yonas, Pola, 64–65
Yonas, Shlomo, 62, 65–67
Youth Aliyah, 35, 72

Zahal (Israel Defense Forces), 50
Zangwill, Israel, 24, 67
Zealots, 86
Zemach, Shlomo, 39, 40
Zichron Ya'akov, 16, 72
Zion, 10, 13, 36
Zionism, 22, 26, 39, 55, 63, 101, 119
Zionist Congress, 44; First, 26, 31, 67; Sixth, 28; 17th, 35; 22nd, 36
Zionists, 16, 26, 44, 45, 55, 113
Zola, Emile, 19